THE
RESUME
HANDBOOK

THE RESUME HANDBOOK

How to Write Outstanding Resumes and Cover Letters for Every Situation

Third Edition

**Arthur D. Rosenberg
& David Hizer**

ADAMS MEDIA CORPORATION
Holbrook, Massachusetts

Dedication

The authors gratefully acknowledge the support and inspiration of our wives, Sara Hizer and Catherine Huang Rosenberg; the efforts of our dear friend of long standing, Harvey Hohauser, in bringing us together; the editorial and graphic assistance of Judy Unruh; and the patience of our editor, Ed Walters.

Published by
Adams Media Corporation
260 Center Street, Holbrook, MA 02343
www.adamsmedia.com

ISBN: 1-55850-616-0

Printed in Canada.

J   I   H   G   F   E

Library of Congress Cataloging-in-Publication Data
Rosenberg, Arthur D.
The resume handbook : how to write outstanding resumes and
cover letters for every situation / Arthur D. Rosenberg & David Hizer. — 3rd ed.
p.   cm.
ISBN 1-55850-616-0 (pbk.)
1. Resumes (Employment). I. Hizer, David V. II. Title.
HF5383.H53   1996
808'.06665—dc20   96-992
                                          CIP

This publication is designed to provide accurate and authoritative information with regard to the subject matter covered. It is sold with the understanding that the publisher is not engaged in rendering legal, accounting, or other professional advice. If legal advice or other expert assistance is required, the services of a competent professional person should be sought.
— From a *Declaration of Principles* jointly adopted by a Committee of the American Bar Association and a Committee of Publishers and Associations

This book is available at quantity discounts for bulk purchases.
For information, call 1-800-872-5627 (in Massachusetts, 617-767-8100).

Visit our exciting small business Web site at businesstown.com

About the Authors

Dave Hizer is a Detroit-based Executive Search Consultant with Harvey Hohauser & Associates who dedicates his time to finding talented executives to match opportunities in his clients' organizations.

With over twenty-five years of experience in executive searches, organizational development, consulting, public speaking, human resources, and outplacement, Hizer reads more resumes in a week than the number of newspaper headlines skimmed by most people in a year. He has authored numerous articles on career planning, self-marketing strategies, and related topics, including "The ABC's of Cover Letters," which appeared in the *Wall Street Journal*'s publication, *The National Business Employment Weekly*.

Despite his full schedule, Hizer somehow finds the time to conduct workshops and seminars on leadership and career/life planning, and to create, design, and publish a variety of educational and inspirational posters.

Art Rosenberg is a New York/New Jersey-based consultant specializing in project management, user-friendly documentation, corporate communications, and training. His major publications include *Manipulative Memos—Control Your Career Through the Medium of the Memo* (Tenspeed Press), *Preparing for a Successful Interview* (McGraw Hill), *Chess for Children and the Young at Heart* (Atheneum), and a number of articles (most recently, "Control Your Career with Memos" in *The National Business Employment Weekly*).

Systems analyst, trainer, translator, and oenophile, Rosenberg is a former textbook publisher, marketing manager, and international resident who continues to provide job- and career-related seminars to both professional and minority groups. His eclectic interests include live opera, slow jazz, tournament chess, candlelight cuisine, good books, and Monday Night Football.

Table of Contents

Preface

The purpose of a resume is to *obtain an interview*.

Your resume is your official representative, a verbal portrait calculated *to arouse an important person's interest in meeting you*.

Your resume is not an autobiographical profile; it's a marketing piece on you. It isn't intended to make people like you or admire you.

Think of your resume as a special tool with one specific purpose: *winning an interview*.

That's right, you've got to go out and *win* your interview, and only the inexperienced and the naïve think otherwise. Your resume is a tool designed to get your foot in the doors of companies where you'd like to work. And if you fail to win the interview, you certainly won't get the job.

But there are other resumes out there in competition with your own. So yours must be at least as good as all the others if you're are to stand an even chance. Of course, if your resume is *better* it may give you the advantage.

To write an interview-winning resume, you need to know what to say, and how to say it. For this, you need *The Resume Handbook*.

Just as the purpose of your resume is to obtain the interview, the purpose of *The Resume Handbook* is to illustrate successful resume techniques.

The Resume Handbook tells you what kind of information to include in your resume, and what to leave out. Then it provides you with the tools and techniques to present your chosen facts in a convincing and engaging manner.

The Resume Handbook will help you *win the interview*.

The rest is up to you!

Introduction

After scrutinizing more than 30,000 resumes throughout our careers in professional recruiting work, a single, recurring impression looms large and dominant in our minds: *too many resumes are poorly written and the overwhelming majority of resumes are overwhelmingly dull!*

Ah, but a veritable work of "art vitae" does happen by on rare occasion, one illuminated with a spark of true, creative thought, and which is pleasing to the eye. Now, if this isn't of itself enough to make our lives exciting, it may at least be interesting to read, and maybe—just perhaps—it will inspire sufficient curiosity to invite the author in for a closer look, which is of course the purpose of a resume.

The purpose of this book is to increase the minute percentage of outstanding resumes, in case we have to read another 30,000 of them prior to retirement.

We've taken pains to avoid the fat and wordy formats to which most books of this kind are prone. Instead, we've tried to heed our own advice on writing resumes by making our book interesting and to the point. *The Resume Handbook* presents the essential ingredients that go into successful resumes, with lucid explanations and the clearest of examples.

You can read through this book in less time than it takes to write a resume, then use it as a reference source when you are ready to begin writing your very own.

We've included a chapter on "The Thirty-one Best Resumes We've Ever Seen." You will quickly learn what makes them so effective, and how to apply their winning techniques to your own purposes. The chapter, "The Five Worst Resumes We've Ever Seen," illustrates some of the pitfalls to be avoided at all costs, and may prove equally instructive.

The Resume Handbook focuses on three major objectives:

- ◆ *Organization:* How to structure and give visual impact to your resume so it immediately captures the reader's attention.

- *The Basic Principles:* What to include and what to leave out of your resume, to avoid wasting the reader's time and running the risk of turning him or her off.

- *Accomplishments:* How to write action-oriented accomplishments by using action verbs, enabling you to represent yourself as a highly motivated achiever.

You'll also find a section on cover letters and another on personal sales *(broadcast)* letters; they are too important to ignore and are an essential part of any job hunting campaign. This new edition includes chapters on networking and other self-marketing strategies, designed to help you get your resume into the right hands. But our emphasis remains on writing resumes that will enable you to present yourself in the most appealing and engaging manner possible, to help you win the interviews you want.

— Art Rosenberg & Dave Hizer

Note: Since the original edition of *The Resume Handbook* was published in 1985, over 200,000 copies have been sold. The feedback we've received suggests that the reason for our book's success lies in its clearly written style, direct and practical advice, and its occasional touch of humor. For a helpful book need not be dull and lifeless, any more than a winning resume.

CHAPTER ONE:
Looking for a New Job

Nearly everyone looks for a job at some time in his or her life. The average American worker does so (according to the U.S. Bureau of Labor Statistics) every 3.6 years; according to the National Bureau of Economic Research, Jane and Joe Average work for ten different employers during their respective life-times. In addition, four out of five job-hunters seek to change careers at least once, and volatility in the job market appears to be growing.

Over 50 million North Americans are currently involved in some sort of career change or transition. Over a third of those now looking for a job are currently employed. Whether this is due to the economy, or the suggestion that a large portion of the working force is underutilized, the fact remains that competition in the job market is fierce.

Chin up, for all is not entirely bleak. Many firms hire nearly as many new workers in a given year as their total number of employees. A construction company with one hundred workers may have to hire as many as two hundred per year, due to enormous turnover. Service firms with as few as twenty-five fulltime employees often need to hire one hundred or more each year in order to maintain a stable staff.

So if you're looking for a job, you are in excellent company. Naturally you need a system if you are to compete successfully, a technique that will give you an advantage. This is where *The Resume Handbook* can help. For whatever job search methods you may use, you'd better have a darned good resume to penetrate the screening processes used by most employers.

What's the Point?
The only valid function of your resume is to get you invited for an interview. It is an advertisement of your skills, experience, and knowledge, presented in their most favorable light.

Your resume precedes you in your job search like an emissary of goodwill. Until you meet the interviewer (if you ever do), the resume is *all* they know of you. Approximately one interview is granted for every 245 resumes received.

Obviously, a mediocre resume will rarely win an interview; a poor one hasn't got a chance!

Research tells us that a piece of advertising matter has about a second and a half in which to attract the reader's interest. Someone sitting with a stack of 245 resumes (and probably a whole lot more) is simply not going to accord them equal time. So why not see to it that yours receives the lion's share of the interviewer's attention?

Read on . . . we'll show you how.

Why Write a Resume If I'm Not Looking For a Job?

Three reasons:

First, the majority of desirable positions are offered to individuals who are employed and who aren't necessarily seeking a new job. You never know when opportunity will knock, when the "job of a lifetime" may dangle within your reach. So, it always pays to have an updated copy of your resume at hand for unexpected opportunities.

The second reason is that it can be a valuable experience to observe one's own professional career on paper. Your resume can put your past experience, growth, and goals into perspective, and help chart the path of your future career.

Finally, having a resume can help protect you from the unexpected, like losing your job in an economic turndown. A well-prepared resume can take some of the anxiety out of the job search, especially for the experienced professional who suddenly finds him- or herself competing for jobs against young professionals who may be better versed in the latest sophisticated job hunting techniques.

Resume Organization

There are three commonly used resume formats:

■ *Chronological* resumes are safe for people with unbroken records of employment. It's a straightforward, easy-to-follow format (see resume examples 1, 2, 4a, 6, 9, 12, 13, 14, 17, 21, 24, 25, and 27 in "The Thirty-one Best Resumes We've Ever Seen") which includes the dates of current and past employment.

■ *Functional* (thematic) resumes, unlike chronological ones, focus rather on accomplishments (see examples 3, 4b, 7, 20, and 31). This format is advisable for those with employment gaps due to unemployment, or other activities they might prefer not to reveal (such as jobs from which they were fired or left after a short time, unsuccessful self-employment, prison terms, and a host of other reasons). It is also a better way to emphasize certain aspects of one's career. If, for example, you spent eleven years teaching engineering and only two years as an industrial engineer, a chronological resume would draw attention to your teaching background. But if you happened to be looking for an engineering position within a corporation, the functional format would allow you to play up your industrial experience and de-emphasize the academic side.

Another rationale for choosing the functional approach is if you haven't much to list by way of experience. This tends to be the case with recent graduates, and those seeking new (or planning to resume) careers after prolonged periods at home.

■ *Combined* chronological/functional resumes can, when appropriate, offer the best of two worlds (see examples 5, 8, 10, 11, 15, 16, 18, 19, 22, 23, 26, 28, 29, and 30).

Each of these resume styles will be demonstrated in intimate detail later in this book. But first:

Resume Preparation

Composing even a brief autobiographical outline requires serious preparation and contemplation. So find a quiet spot (office, den, or dining room table) where you feel comfortable and can be alone and undisturbed. Set aside a period of four to five hours and, if possible, unplug the phone.

Collect all the materials you will need, including:

- ◆ Pens, pencils, or both—whatever you like using best
- ◆ A lined pad (at least 8½" x 11")
- ◆ A good dictionary and a thesaurus
- ◆ Records of your past employment, education, and related materials
- ◆ Copies of former job applications and correspondence, if available
- ◆ Descriptions of some jobs for which you plan to apply
- ◆ A copy of *The Resume Handbook*

Now that you're suitably equipped, you can begin to formulate your own *resume strategy*. Be careful to observe the basic principles of resume writing, which follow next.

CHAPTER TWO:
The Basic Principles of Resume Writing

Writing a successful resume is an art, with certain basic principles that should be kept in mind. The following suggestions have been formulated through long years of exposure to all sorts of resumes. Major deviations from these "rules" are at your own creative—and professional—risk.

■ *Brief is better!* See if you can fit it all on a single page (especially recent graduates and those early in their careers), but don't exceed two pages. Remember, few executives enjoy the task of reading piles of resumes, let alone the thick, voluminous monsters that get mailed out every day. A potential exception to this rule is the consultant's resume, which may need to list one's technical skills, projects, and clients comprehensively. (See resume example 31 in Chapter Four.)

■ *Format:* Your name (in bold type or in capital letters), address, and both home and work telephone numbers belong on top. Next come your objectives and summary of qualifications, accomplishments, employment history, education, and related activities and affiliations. Select the resume from "The Thirty-one Best Resumes We've Ever Seen" that most closely meets your needs and suits your style, and use it as a model, or combine elements from several of these resume samples.

Education may precede employment history in certain cases, especially if a recent graduate or technical degree is more closely related to the desired position than your employment history. Recent graduates, with little or no work experience, have little choice.

■ *Optional categories:* These may include career objectives, summary of qualifications, and such personal details as date of birth, marital status, military record, and health. Let's take a separate look at each of these:

◆ *Career Objectives:* This can be an excellent topic to include if you happen to possess a clear idea of what they are. But general or vague objectives are best omitted. Remember, your objectives can be honed specifically to the job for which you are applying in your cover letter, which we'll address a little later.

Your career objectives must be worded with precision if they are to be included in your resume. They should be clearly stated and consistent with your accomplishments and demonstrated skills, as documented on your resume. Bear in mind the difference between career and job objectives. A career objective is just that . . . a long-range plan that may or may not relate directly to the job for which your are applying. A job objective, on the other hand, is oriented quite specifically to the opening you wish to fill. We recommend using the term "objective" by itself, which would be appropriate for most situations.

♦ *Summary of Qualifications:* A detailed resume that includes a wealth of professional experience can employ this effectively. The summary may be inserted in addition to, or instead of, a statement of objectives; or the two can be combined ("qualifications and objectives"). At its best, a summary will entice the reader to read further; at its worst, it has the opposite effect. A summary is most helpful if the applicant has had an extremely diversified background, including (for instance) teaching and industry (see "The Thirty-one Best"), or if the resume extends beyond a single page. An effective and well-written summary attracts the reader's eye, brings the essence of your resume into focus, and compels the reader to move on to the main details.

♦ *Personal Data:* If your personal details are "Mom-and-apple pie" and straight as the proverbial arrow, they may lend an air of respectability to your image. However, any nonessential information that you offer is more likely to work against you. Let's face it, prejudices do exist (for example) toward single women, unmarried men over a certain age, and older job-seekers—and why should *anyone* advertise that they're divorced? Your date of birth may only serve to persuade potential employers that you are too young or too old for a given job before they've even met you. Your military record may be worth mentioning if it includes some sort or relevant job training or experience (technical, organizational; see Abel Baker's resume in "The Thirty-one Best"). And finally, who on earth would admit in writing to poor physical (or mental) health? Omit *any* reference to health.

■ Also leave out:

♦ Reasons for having left a job—they won't enhance your image, and you may create a negative impression.

- Former (or desired) salary—you need to know as much as possible about the job in order to avoid asking for too little or too much. Don't risk putting yourself out of the running before you've even begun.

- Hobbies and memberships in social, fraternal, or religious organizations—potential employers don't need this information, and you never know what may turn them off.

- Reasons for *not* having served in the military.

- Any potentially negative information about you (unless unavoidable), such as prison terms, lost lawsuits, and handicaps that may affect your job performance.

- The label "Resume" or "Vitae"—if the briefest glance does not clearly identify your resume as such, the label will not help.

- The banal "References available on request"; this is taken for granted.

■ *Visual impact:* Use the same type style throughout your resume, and use bold, italics, or all caps for headings and emphasis (as discussed in Chapter Six). Do not send out photocopies; spend a few dollars to have your resume professionally printed or use a high-quality laser printer . . . the difference is well worth the cost. Always print your resume on quality paper. As clothes make the woman or man, cheap-looking paper will detract from your resume. Stick with white, off-white, or light shades of beige or gray. Make sure the resume is *letter-perfect*. Errors, typos, stains, abbreviations (*etc., e.g., i.e.*), technical jargon, and hip or buzz words are strictly taboo. Get your final draft critiqued and proofread by someone reliable.

■ *Ensure integrity:* Poorly written resumes typically lack internal integrity; yours should be consistent. Your job or career objective (if you use one) will be supported by the accomplishments you list. If you are interested in a senior position with an advertising firm, then you should emphasize your accomplishments in management, business development, and in creative programs you've developed. If you include a "Summary of Qualifications" section, it must represent in brief the rest of your resume. If not, you will confuse the reader. The bottom line here is that your resume provides separate—but interrelated—facts.

■ *Employment history:* When writing a chronological resume, strike a balance between job content and accomplishments; the latter should be emphasized (as we'll explain in the next chapter). List your current position first, working back chronologically. De-emphasize the jobs you held further back in time. Avoid verifiable exaggerations that may someday constitute grounds for dismissal, but do use action verbs and phrases to best present the facts to your advantage (see Chapter Three).

Here's an example of a balanced job history:

1989 to present	Flinthall Electronics, Dover, Ohio. Manager of product testing. Supervise testing group consisting of seven research engineers. Group's mission was to create methods to test performance, safety, and durability characteristics of projected products. While heading up this group: • Initiated testing methods that reduced annual budget of group by 20%. • Received award of excellence for innovations in testing by *American Society of Research Engineers*—1990. • Increased group efficiency as measured by time and quantity parameters by 35%. • Developed three patented testing procedures during last four years.

In the above example, the first paragraph clarifies the job's content—what was supposed to be done. This introduction sets up and brings clarity to the accomplishments.

■ *Organizations of which you are a member:* You may safely list the ones that show achievement or professional standing, such as the National Association of Certified Public Accountants, or the Tool & Diemaker's Guild. You can also indicate your leadership abilities as an officer or official in a strictly non-controversial association, like the PTA or Junior Achievement. But stay away from listing political, religious, and potentially controversial groups, because they simply don't belong on resumes.

■ *Awards:* Be sure to list awards that relate to the kind of job you're seeking, like Pulitzer Prizes, Oscars, or honorary doctorates. Leave out references to having won the league bowling or karate championship. While these achievements may bolster your ego, they can create uncertain images in the mind of the interviewer. In addition, they have nothing to do with the task at hand— winning an interview.

■ ■ ■

With these basic resume strategy guidelines in mind, it's time now to focus on the specifics of making *your* resume stand out from the other 244.

CHAPTER THREE:
Stating Your Accomplishments

The *manner* in which you state your accomplishments is no less important than the details themselves. Active, energetic phrases attract more of the reader's attention than do dull or passive words. *Created*, for example, sounds more interesting than *began*; *promoted*, *instituted*, and *produced* are much more attention-getting than *worked on*, *became*, or *finished*.

In fact, the very first word you use to describe an accomplishment can make the difference between an impressive resume, and one that's just ho-hum. It may make the difference between its being read or "filed." So before presenting the mechanics of stating your accomplishments in their best possible light, let's pause to digest "Hizer's 57"—a list of action verbs that show you are an *action person*, the kind employers notice.

Hizer's 57
Action Verbs

achieved	directed	organized
administered	eliminated	planned
advanced	established	prepared
advised	evaluated	produced
analyzed	expanded	promoted
authored	focused	provided
automated	headed up	published
coached	identified	reduced
conceptualized	implemented	researched
conducted	improved	restructured
contained	increased	reversed
contracted	initiated	saved
controlled	innovated	scheduled
coordinated	instituted	solved
created	introduced	streamlined
cut	led	supervised
decreased	maintained	taught
designed	managed	trained
developed	negotiated	trimmed

"Hizer's 57" does not pretend to be a complete list of action verbs. These words can, however, be applied to virtually any field or industry, actively demonstrating why your skills would be an asset to any employer. They also help to circumvent the danger of using buzz words, tech-talk, and the like.

Now that you're armed with effective action verbs, it's time to turn them into action phrases that best demonstrate your accomplishments.

Action Phrases

Dull resumes tend to contain a lot of statements and descriptions that appear to have been copied directly from corporate personnel files. This, of course, is poor resume strategy. A better tactic is to employ phrases stressing your accomplishments in such a way as to attract—and hold—the reader's attention.

An interview-winning resume contains a balance of job content and accomplishments. It also has attention-getting style. You may refer to this as flair, technique, or pizzazz . . . in *The Resume Handbook*, we call it *impact*.

To illustrate the point, here are some contrasting examples of statements often found in resumes. Those on the left are dull; in addition, they tell only half the story: what was done. The action phrases on the right, on the other hand, present a larger context in which to evaluate accomplishments more fully. And they are, indeed, more interesting to read, due in large measure to their effective use of action verbs.

Dull	With Impact
1. Raised level of sales above previous year.	1. Reversed negative sales trend; sales up 41% over prior year.
2. Started new employee programs that lowered turnover.	2. Created and implemented two new employee relations programs (flex-time and job posting) resulting in a 33% reduction in turnover.
3. Handled bookings for elderly pop group.	3. Managed bookings, travel, and accommodations for sexagenarian sextet.
4. Housewife of household with six people for past seven years.	4. Managed and organized six-member household with annual budget of $65,000.
5. Marketed new travel plan to corporations, increasing sales $19 million.	5. Initiated new market concept of packaging travel to corporations for incentive programs, resulting in sales of $19 million (more than double expectations).
6. Worked for losing gubernatorial candidate for six months.	6. Organized and coordinated political campaign for leading gubernatorial candidate.

7. Opened new sales offices in two cities that broke quotas ahead of schedule.	7. Researched feasibility, then established two new sales offices; both operated above sales quotas within two years (six months ahead of schedule).
8. Hired and trained six new lion tamers during 1993–1994. Only one serious casualty.	8. Recruited, trained, and motivated six new lion tamers during 1993–1994; five continue to excel.
9. Lowered operating costs in my division by $135,000.	9. Initiated cost reducing plan in my division, resulting in 27% ($135,000) cost reduction with no negative effect on production capability.
10. Put on training sessions for supervisors in corporation.	10. Conducted leadership training for forty-eight supervisory and management level staff members.
11. Increased sales and profitability despite lower budget.	11. Expanded market penetration sales by 14%, and profitability during a period of budgetary cutbacks.
12. Contributed to making group much more efficient.	12. Increased group efficiency as measured by time and quantity parameters by 35%.
13. Wrote ornithology procedures manual for museum.	13. Conceptualized and authored eighty-eight-page ornithology procedures manual for museum zoological research department.

In many of the preceding examples, you'll notice a relationship between the action verb used in the phrases with impact, and a more complete and detailed description of accomplishments. This is because action verbs invite further questions—even from you as you are reflecting on your achievements and writing your resume.

Focus on accomplishments that had a noticeable or measurable effect on some part of the place where you worked. Use the following list of questions to stimulate your recollection of what you accomplished.

1. Were you able to increase sales? Did you meet or break goals, quotas, or expectations?

2. Did you cut losses or save money? Did you retain a key account or customer?

3. Did you identify and solve important problems? Don't dismiss what you consider obvious; it may be a critical issue to someone else.

4. Did you install a new system or procedure? Include an indication of time lines, cost consciousness, or quality results.

5. Have you reengineered procedures? What were the results?

6. Did you demonstrate your willingness to be a team player?

7. Have you shown leadership skills? Show how and what resulted.

8. Have you trained others to meet or surpass expectations? What training techniques did you use?

9. Did you suggest any new services or products? What resulted?

10. Have you acted as a coordinator, liaison, representative, or committee member in any capacity that made a difference? What difference did it make?

11. Have you demonstrated a willingness to assume extra responsibilities or work?

12. Have you accomplished anything that was considered difficult or impossible?

13. Can you show a record of consistency and reliability? (Example: completing projects on time.)

14. Have you ever cleaned up someone else's mess?

15. Have you performed independently without close supervision? What were the results?

16. Have you ever gone way out of your way to provide exceptional service to a client or customer? What happened as a result?

17. Has your work performance been recognized by a superior? Why? What did you do?

18. Have you ever been told by a peer, superior, supplier, or customer that you made a big difference? What was the result of the difference?

19. What was the most extraordinary, fulfilling, and professionally satisfying thing you've ever done? What resulted?

A careful blend of action verbs and specific accomplishments will get the interviewer's attention. It may motivate him or her to call you in for a serious interview.

Take a look at the following examples and think about your own accomplishments:

- *Successfully managed*, for past eleven years, a five-member household with an annual budget of $59,200, while completing Associate of Business degree at Clinton Valley Community College.

- *Researched, wrote and published* information booklet for graduating college seniors: "Don't Pass Go, Don't Collect Up To $200,000 Now."

- *Conceptualized and founded* Meadow Lane Day Care Center, which now cares for twenty-nine children daily.

- *Controlled* expenses on "Parents March for M.S."; treasurer for Imperial and Essex Counties.

- *Organized* food cooperative that purchased $119,000 in consumables during 1992.

- *Created* children's tee-shirt design, then implemented marketing program resulting in gross sales in excess of $70,000.

- *Maintained* 3.9 grade average in business courses at Ohio State University. Completed eleven courses to date.

- *Elected* to represent Nevada State University at the International Congress on Energy Alternatives in Prague.

- *Chosen* over thirty-seven other trainees by senior management as member of four-person management trainee group organized to rewrite the training program we had just taken.

- *Created* neighborhood theatre ensemble which, over the last nine years, has developed into the nationally renowned "Westgate Orchards Theatre Ensemble."

- *Written up* in *Oregon's Eye O-U* (alumni newspaper) as one of ten most promising freshmen in 1996.

- *Initiated* and headed up ninety-member "Students for Intellectual Expansion"—University of Missouri's answer to President Carter's challenge to create alternative energy.

- *Conducted* sensitive quality control study for Southeast Michigan Water Authority—written up in Michigan Congressional Record, June 1994, "Standing Ovation for H_2O."

- *Formed* local Junior Chamber of Commerce, which has grown from nineteen to 291 members.

- *Elected* to Board of Directors of the $36 million asset Tri-County Employees Credit Union.

- *Originated* and published *Salescall*, an informational newsletter distributed to 144 sales representatives throughout the U.S. *Salescall* covers sales techniques, product knowledge, legislative updates, notes of competition, and technical changes.

- *Headed up* procedures group that eliminated nineteen obsolete reports and modified, or combined, fourteen others (out of a total of forty-nine) without reducing operational effectiveness.

- *Designed* assembly pivot arm that increased overall line speed by 9%, resulting in an increase in daily production of thirty-nine units (15% increase).

- *Produced* videotape program entitled "Here to Help," outlining Marcot's product servicing capabilities to current and prospective clients.

- *Instituted* self-developed safety program within my production wing of 179 employees, resulting in lost work day savings of 39% over previous three years.

The preceding accomplishment statements are action-oriented because they start with action verbs. The statements are achievement-oriented in that they demonstrate the writer's capability of organizing, completing, leading, and doing. They accomplish this by:

Using quantitative measures to emphasize to what extent the writer completed that achievement. Example: Scored in the 95th percentile on seven out of the eight-part state licensing exam for electricians.

Using position to indicate the relative importance of the achievement. Example: Awarded second place out of sixty entrants in the National Collegiate Debate Association "Debate 94" in St. Louis.

Using action verbs to indicate selection over others. Example: Selected fifth for the presupervisory awareness program at Big Sky Electric out of 195 candidates.

Using action verbs to indicate leadership in creating, initiating or heading an activity of group. Example: Organized and was first chairperson of Moravia Valley Glass and Can Reclamation Center, which collected 119 tons of recyclable glass and aluminum during 1995. Example: Organized and led 36-member church bazaar group that successfully raised $28,760 over a two-year period.

For Students and the Newly Graduated

A special note to students, new graduates, and those returning to work after a lengthy absence: Remember to look outside the work arena in developing your accomplishment statements. With limited or outdated work experience, you need to explore your personal experiences for ways to sell yourself to a potential employer.

1. Consider writing about your membership and leadership involvement in campus clubs and organizations. Avoid mentioning controversial or unsanctioned groups.

Example: "Captained intramural coed softball team that won campus championship, 1994. Recruited, coached, and motivated fourteen players."

2. Look for an accomplishment statement in a term project or paper that you wrote. This is especially advantageous if it relates to your job objective or career interest.

   Example: "Researched and wrote twenty-one-page term paper, entitled *Which Niche Now*, that listed the latest approaches in identifying and appealing to your product's market. (Received an 'A.')"

3. Form an accomplishment statement around a noteworthy comment made by a professor, instructor, or teacher that shows your creativity, insight, or hard work.

   Example: "Recognized verbally by organic chemistry professor who stated that I had 'natural research instincts' and I was 'bound for greater heights'."

4. Include accomplishment statements that show initiative and responsibility.

   Example: "Initiated, organized, and led almost entire dormitory population in preparing for Parents' Day–June 1995. Parents were overwhelmingly united in their praise of the day's events."

5. Think in terms of specialized training and learning experiences that exhibit uniqueness or an interest in learning new things.

   Example: "Volunteered to stay after hours and without pay to learn and work with employer's bookkeeper in closing out the financial books; subsequently closed out next month's books on own—without pay."

For Those Returning to Work After an Absence

1. Include volunteer work—school, civil, or community.

   Example: "Selected by Lancaster County School Board as 'Volunteer of the Year,' 1992; finished second in 1993."

2. Identify how hobbies might provide material showing uniqueness or expertise.

   Example: "Featured in *Furniture Refinishing* magazine (April 1994) for volunteer work teaching high school sophomores and juniors furniture repair and refinishing."

3. Show how you have found ways to keep your skills updated.

   Example: "Established home-based research and advisory service using Internet resources to provide corporate clients with recent patent and copyright filings."

4. Explore how managing family issues can serve as work-relevant accomplishments.

   Example: "Conducted exhaustive research that led to identifying a rare learning disorder that doctors and clinicians had been unable to diagnose. Identification led to successful treatment and article in *Parents* magazine entitled 'How Parents Can Make a Difference.'"

5. Consider how continuing education (including self-development) shows your initiative and sense of responsibility.

   Example: "During 1992–1994 completed three Dale Carnegie courses on Sales, Leadership, and Public Speaking. Named top graduate in leadership program."

Describing Your Education

If your employment experience is limited, your educational background may be more relevant to the job you're seeking. In this case, your education will be the initial accomplishment you list. (See examples in the next chapter.) Regardless of whether it is your key accomplishment or subordinate to your job history, there are methods of presenting your educational background concisely and impressively.

For an individual with extensive employment experience, it is usually sufficient to list the bare details:

> 1990: B.S., Biology, Howard University, Washington, D.C.

or

> Cornell University, Ithaca, N.Y.: M.B.A., Business Administration

You may, of course, list any academic honors earned:

> 1992: San Diego State University, San Diego, California: M.A., History *(cum laude)*.

or

> University of New Hampshire, 1994: B.A. in Fine Arts; graduated *summa cum laude*.

If your employment experience is limited, it is a good idea to elaborate on educational achievements before employment:

> 1996—Bachelor of Arts Degree in Business Administration, University of Florida. Achieved 3.6 grade average (4.0 scale); specialized in management information systems. Senior project consisted of 223-page report on the compatibility of selected information retrieval systems. Excerpts were published in July 1993 edition of *M.I.S.*

or

> Boston University, College of Communication, 1987. Maintained 3.5/4.0 GPA; emphasized newspaper journalism sequence. While in school, served as editor of *The Daily Free Press* (1994–95); awarded John Scali Achievement Prize for best student investigative news story.

If you have extensive relevant work experience in an academic setting (as do researchers, law students, journalism students, and others), be sure to carefully describe that work with action phrases. Limited employment experience also necessitates creativity in describing other educational achievements. A lecture heard at college, work, or elsewhere may be described as:

> December 1992: Attended seminar on "Business Computer Languages" at RETI School of Electronics, Rapid City, SD.

or

> Summer 1988: Participated in week-long seminar on publishing procedures and marketing techniques, University of New Mexico.

List any relevant certificates you've earned:

> Received "Fortran Programming Proficiency" certificate from ABC Business Institute, Phoenix, AZ: February, 1994.

or

> Awarded certificate of proficiency in "Business Communication Machinery" from Control Info Institute, 1993.

If you lack a college degree, emphasize any classes attended or years completed. This can be worded so as to reflect that you're in the process of completing a degree:

> *UNIVERSITY OF MIAMI (Evening Division)*: B.S., Mathematics; in progress.

or

> Currently working toward B.S. Degree in Public Administration, University of Delaware.

People with a lot of professional experience commonly list the seminars, lectures, or certificate programs they have attended, and so should you. This will help to mitigate any negative impressions your lack of a degree might create.

Those who haven't earned college degrees are advised to list their high school diplomas. For example:

Diploma (with honors), Davis High School, Mt. Vernon, N.Y.

or

Graduated (college preparatory courses) Edgewater High School, Orlando, FL.

■ ■ ■

Following these guidelines on stating your accomplishments, your resume should fairly sing to an employer: *Call me in for an interview; I can help your company*. Remember, your resume is all they know of you until you walk through that door. The only way an employer can identify you as an action-oriented individual is from your resume, and action verbs will help you to accomplish this objective.

Having mastered the art of using action verbs, your remaining task is a mechanical one: plugging these action phrases into the following general format.

When stating your accomplishments, be sure to include:

- ◆ Name and location of the organization (city/state only; street address is unnecessary)
- ◆ Specific job title
- ◆ Job description
- ◆ Skills applied
- ◆ Skills acquired (if applicable)
- ◆ Significant accomplishments
- ◆ Dates of employment (unless using functional format)

In listing former jobs, it is recommended that you go back no more than ten to twelve years, unless you've spent all that time with the same company; in that case, briefly list an earlier job or two.

Gaps in employment dates of more than a month or two should, if possible, be "hidden" (or briefly explained, e.g., sabbatical to complete degree, illness, military service, etc.) by extending dates of earlier and later employment, or even better, by employing a functional format.

Once you've stated your accomplishments using action verbs and phrases that embellish your performance, you've completed the most difficult part of writing an effective resume.

Ready to begin? Before you do, we suggest you take a look at Chapters Four and Five, to see how others have created their masterpieces . . . and disasters.

CHAPTER FOUR:
The Thirty-one Best Resumes We've Ever Seen

The following resumes, appropriately edited and modified (in order to conceal the identity of the authors), are among the best we've yet discovered. Selected from more than thirty thousand resumes inspected over a period of years, these examples pull together the various techniques we've been discussing. Each one deals with a specific, real-life situation. There are examples here for just about every situation, and there are elements from each that you may want to consider incorporating into yours.

These thirty-one resumes are organized into the three categories we looked at earlier:

- ◆ Chronological: This type of resume is fairly straightforward; eleven examples are included (see resume examples 1, 2, 4a, 6, 9, 12, 13, 14, 17, 21, 24, 25 and 27).

- ◆ Functional: This category allows for a great deal of variation (see resume examples 3, 4b, 7, 20, and 31).

- ◆ Combined: Here we apply the best of both techniques (see resume examples 5, 8, 10, 11, 15, 16, 18, 19, 22, 23, 26, 28, 29, and 30).

Good work speaks for itself, so we present these exemplary resumes intact. The concepts that make each of them stand out are noted in the margins.

Each resume is labeled by format (chronological, functional, combined) and general background of the user. Nevertheless, they are intended to serve as good examples of just about any career-oriented resume, and the lessons from each can be applied to your own uses.

■ ■ ■

Resume Example #1: An imaginative and creative "blue-collar professional" looking for a better job.

PIERRE CUISINE
MASTER CHEF

14 Fourchette Boulevard

Telephone (mornings)

New Orleans, Louisiana

(304) 555-0544

The proper blend of training and diversified experience is my recipe for culinary excellence!

From the everyday to the extraordinary. After your clientele have tasted my international entrees they will demand an "encore."

> CREATIVE OBJECTIVE FOR A CREATIVE BUSINESS

EXPERIENCE

1993 - Present   **ARNAUD'S RESTAURANT**   **HEAD CHEF**
New Orleans, Louisiana
Manage entire kitchen staff of twenty-two that produces the finest luncheons and dinners in the South.

> EVIDENCE OF MANAGEMENT ABILITIES AND EXPERIENCE

- Create extraordinary seafood, meat, and chicken dishes, specializing in delicate sauces.
- Supervise three assistant chefs and wine steward.
- Oversee training of four apprentices.
- Responsible for purchases of all foods and kitchen budget of $1.4 million.

1989 - 1993   **LE CHATEAU**   **CHEF**
Charlesbourg, Quebec
One of two chefs directly under head chef

- Prepared special sauces and such delicate specialties as pheasant under glass.
- Served flambées and other spectacular dishes in dining room.
- Conceived and wrote all lunch menus.

1985 - 1989   **CHEZ PAUL BEAUCOUP**   **APPRENTICE CHEF**
Paris, France

- Prepared hors d'oeuvres, entrees, and desserts under the direction of one of the world's foremost chefs.
- Assisted in the purchase of foods and kitchen supplies.

EDUCATION
1985

Diploma, École d'Haute Cuisine, Lyons, France
Generally recognized as the leading cooking school in Europe.

> THE TYPE OF TRAINING THAT STANDS OUT

SPECIAL TALENTS

- Capable of serving as knowledgeable wine steward.
- Fluent French and English; spoken Italian and Spanish.
- Aware of kosher dietary laws.

PERSONAL

> MAKES AN IMPORTANT POINT THAT MIGHT OTHERWISE BE OVERLOOKED

- Dual nationality: French and Canadian.
- Willing to relocate anywhere in the world.

> CLEVER, WITTY, APPEALING

CHRONOLOGICAL

Resume Example #2: Administrative professional with solid office skills and a record of steady employment.

FRANCIS L. WORKLIFE

1404 MOORE AVENUE
LINCOLN, MISSOURI 65338

HOME: (417) 555-4771

PROFESSIONAL SUMMARY

Administrative office professional with eleven years of progressively more challenging assignments. Strong computer skills in applications including word processing, spreadsheet, database, graphics, and accounting. Capable of rapidly learning new assignments involving decision making, organization of data, customer service, working cross-functionally with others, and prioritizing responsibilities. Responsible, reliable, and able to work quickly and accurately.

TECHNICAL/OFFICE SKILLS

SOFTWARE   Microsoft Office (Word, Excel, Powerpoint, Access); Wordperfect; Lotus 1-2-3; Foxpro; Amipro. Can adapt and learn any new software.

HARDWARE   Have worked on a variety of PCs and Macintosh; proficient in both DOS and Windows environments.

WORK HISTORY

1991 to PRESENT   **UNION CARBONS; Lincoln, Nebraska**
Secretary and Administrative Assistant to Vice President in Charge of Sales.
Duties include: Preparing sales reports and basic market research reports. Scheduling travel arrangements for nine sales professionals. Supervising two other clerical assistants. Ensuring that all filing, letters, and reports produced by department meet quality standards for timeliness, clarity, and accuracy.

1986 to 1991   **HANSON, MARKUM, AND ROBB; Lincoln, Nebraska**
Senior Secretary to Managing Partners of a seventeen-partner CPA firm.
Duties included: Overseeing all internal accounting for hours worked and billed. Supervising one other clerical assistant. Preparing minutes for all weekly partner meetings. Maintaining partner business development reporting and tracking. Maintaining all personnel files for firm's twenty-nine employees. Recruiting and hiring all clerical/administrative personnel.

1984 to 1986   **SECOND NATIONAL BANK; Lincoln, Nebraska**
Secretary, Commercial Loan Department
Duties included: Typing of all loan documents and departmental correspondence. Maintaining Loan Committee notes. Greeting and directing all guests.

EDUCATION and TRAINING

Evelyn Steel Secretarial School Lincoln, Nebraska   Received diploma and Top Student Award for eighteen-month program, 1988.

Xerox Training Center St. Louis, Missouri   Certificate of proficiency for Basic PC Training, 1988.

PERSONAL

Enjoy travel, willing to relocate.

CHRONOLOGICAL

Resume Example #3: High-tech!

MIKE ROCHIP

3390 Disk Drive
Silicon Valley, Georgia 30314

Residence: (404) 555-2628
Business: (404) 555-9284

OBJECTIVE

SOLID OBJECTIVE

To provide systems programming services in a major DP complex; to upgrade the skills of systems programming staff through specialized training.

SUMMARY

STRONG CREDENTIALS

Over twenty years of data processing experience encompassing all aspects of operating systems: Installation, Service, Diagnostics, Design, Development, Testing, Build/Integration, Project Leadership, Prototyping, Research, Education, and Consulting.

HARDWARE:

IBM ES/9000, 303x, 308x, 4341, 4381, IBM PC.

IMPRESSIVE TECHNICAL KNOWLEDGE AND SKILLS

SOFTWARE:

MVS/ESA, VSE/ESA, MVS/XA, MVS/SP, VM/370, TSO, CMS, ISPF, SMP/E, JES2, JES3, VSAM BDAM, IMS, RACF, ICF, IDCAMS, DF/EF, RMF, DFP, IPCS, NJE, IPO/SIPO, CBIPO, OMEGAMON, SAM-E, VTAM, TCAM, DB2.

LANGUAGES:

S/370 BAL, PL/1, APL, BASIC, PASCAL, REXX, FORTRAN, COBOL II, COBOL/370.

ACTION WORDS TELL WHAT HE'S DONE

PROFESSIONAL ACHIEVEMENTS

Design:
Wrote design specifications for major components of three operating systems.

Development:
Led technical team in development of major MVS component.

Prototyping:
Designed, coordinated, and implemented 20K LOC prototype for major component of MVS.

Negotiation:
Coordinated design efforts and strategic directions of four IBM divisions for a major VM component.

Testing:
Wrote, coordinated, and tracked component test plan for MVS Supervisor (OS/VS2 Release 2).

Integration:
Served as key technical planner in development of build plan for OS/VS2 Release (MVS).

Installation:
Converted three data centers from MVS/XA to MVS/ESA.

Maintenance:
Installed and serviced the following major systems and system components:

ACHIEVEMENTS CLEARLY CATEGORIZED

MVS/XA	MVS/SP	VM/370	IMS/VS
TSO/E	VTAM	JES2	JES3
RACF	DFP	DF/EF	TCAM
ISPF	NJE	RMF	3270/Session Mgr.
TSO	DMS/OS	APL/SV	

MEANINGFUL DETAILS TO TECHNICAL EMPLOYERS

and numerous additional program products.

FUNCTIONAL

Planning:	Specified and justified hardware/software systems in support of growth and changing demands of education department for IBM's Data Systems Division.
Tuning:	• Supervised performance measurement and tuning of MVS Installation containing interactive (IMS, TSO, APL/SV, and IIS) and batch. Accomplished both in a native and VM production guest environment.
	• Led division task force to reduce path length in paging-related components of MVS (OS/VS2 Release 2); impacted five system components, resulted in path-length reduction in excess of 25%.
	• Headed IBM corporate task force to solve MVS V2CR problem.
Instruction:	• Created and taught courses in languages, DB/DC, operating systems, teleprocessing, and system diagnostics.
	• Designed/developed productivity-enhancing software tools.

A SPECIAL CATEGORY OF EXPERIENCE

- • IMS to TSO interface (Interactive DL/1).
- • Full-screen editor for IBM 2250.
- • Created interactive system of programs to plan, model, and schedule.
- • Designed and taught seminars on effective use of visual aids (videotaped and used as standard training aid for IBM instructors and managers).
- • Developed and taught electronics specialty upgrade courses for SAC headquarters electronics technicians.

Technical Publications:	• "MVS-VM/370 Cohabitation—Making the Marriage Work"
	• "Dynamic Generation and Control of Large Data Bases for Interactive Systems Testing"
	• "Large System Effects in MVS"
	• Cache Cross-Interrogate Effects in an N-Way MVS System"
Software Patents:	• "Dynamic Quickcell Function"—status = file

THE ICING ON THE CAKE

EDUCATION:	• Clemson University M.A. - Systems Analysis 1981
	• Georgia Tech B.A. - Mathematics 1977

Resume Example #4a: *A former academic who made the jump into the world of business.*

V. KING BRACE

42 Community Circle
Orlando, Florida 32801

Home: (904) 555-4090
Office: (904) 555-9409

EMPLOYMENT EXPERIENCE

5/91 - Present

Barfield & Ivanovich, Inc.   **Senior Editor of**
Orlando, Florida   **Social Studies and History**
Acquisition and publication of professional reference textbooks.

COST SAVINGS

- Cancelled 20 outdated and unwanted contracts without expense or litigation, saving an estimated $500,000.
- Revamped existing list of social studies texts, more than doubling revenue over a two-year period.
- Established and published a profitable selection of history books, leading to the creation of a new Assistant Editor position.

8/86 - 5/91

Hazard House Publishing   **Social Sciences Editor**
New York, New York
Acquisition and publication of college textbooks.   SPECIFIC ACHIEVEMENTS

- Redefined short- and medium-range publishing priorities in fields of psychology and sociology.
- Increased profitability of list by 44% during a period of budget reductions.

MANAGERIAL ACHIEVEMENT

- Improved communications between editorial and sales staff, resulting in largest single-year sales increase in eleven years.

9/82 - 8/86

New York University   **Assistant Professor of Psychology**
New York, New York

- Conducted graduate and undergraduate classes in behavioral and clinical psychology.
- Initiated liaisons between department and college publishing houses, resulting in fifty to sixty graduate students serving as management reviewers.

ACADEMIC

**RELATED
PROFESSIONAL
ACTIVITIES**

- Consultant to Hazard House Publishing Company while teaching at New York University.
- Advisor to New York State Behavioral Research Center.

CHRONOLOGICAL

The Resume Handbook

PUBLICATIONS

| RELEVANT TO ACADEMIA |
| AND PUBLISHING |

1992: *Behavior in an Industrial Society* (with Dr. I. H. Feuerbach), Barfield & Ivanovich.

1989: *The Inhuman Time Bomb* (edited readings), Irving Press.

1980 - 1988: Twenty-two articles and monographs in professional journals (including *The Behaviorist*) and popular publications (including *Psychology Tomorrow*).

EDUCATION

1981: Ph.D., Clinical Psychology, University of California at Los Angeles

1977: M.A., Industrial Psychology, Kent State University, Kent, Ohio

1976: B.A., Psychology, Youngstown State University, Youngstown, Ohio

FOREIGN LANGUAGES

German   **COULD DELETE**

Resume Example #4b: Here is the same person as in #4a, but with his background presented in a functional format.

V. KING BRACE

42 Community Circle
Orlando, Florida 32801

Home: (904) 555 4090
Office: (904) 555-9409

OBJECTIVE

The editorial directorship of a major social sciences and humanities publishing department in higher education.

> TO THE POINT

SUMMARY OF QUALIFICATIONS

Over six years of highly successful editorial acquisitions, including extensive experience in: product development, planning, budgeting, marketing, management, staff supervision, and training, with Barfield and Ivanovich (Orlando) and Hazard House (New York).

> EMPHASIZES PUBLISHING BACKGROUND

PROFESSIONAL ACHIEVEMENTS

Product Development
- Published highly profitable selection of academic textbooks, increasing revenue by more than 100% (over a two-year period) and increasing profitability by 44% (during a period of budget cutbacks).

> COMPLETE STATEMENT

Planning and Budgeting
- Established editorial priorities for one- and five-year plans, including budget requirements and projected revenues.
- Saved an estimated $500,000 by cancelling outdated and unwanted contracts without expense or litigation.

> ACCOMPLISHMENTS ARE PLACED IN A MEANINGFUL CONTEXT

Marketing
- Produced accurate and meaningful data for marketing and sales staff, contributing to exceptionally high sales increase.

Management Supervision and Training
- Coordinated workflow of copy and production editors, publishing schedules, and daily interaction with more than 25 authors.
- Supervised two junior acquisitions editors, both of whom were subsequently promoted.
- Implemented visible and successful on-the-job training program for editorial assistants.

RELATED PROFESSIONAL ACTIVITIES
- Assistant Professor of Psychology, New York University
- Consultant to Hazard House (while teaching)
- Advisor to New York State Behavioral Research Center

> DOWNPLAYS ACADEMIC BACKGROUND

FUNCTIONAL

The Resume Handbook

PUBLICATIONS

1992: *Behavior in an Industrial Society* (with Dr. I. H. Feuerbach), Barfield & Ivanovich.
1989: *The Inhuman Time Bomb* (edited readings), Irving Press.
1980 - 1988: Twenty-two articles and monographs in professional journals (including *The Behaviorist*) and popular publications (including *Psychology Tomorrow*).

EDUCATION

1981: Ph.D., Clinical Psychology, University of California at Los Angeles
1977: M.A., Industrial Psychology, Kent State University, Kent, Ohio
1976: B.A., Psychology, Youngstown State University, Youngstown, Ohio

FOREIGN LANGUAGES

German

OUACHITA TECHNICAL COLLEGE

Resume Example #5: Leaving the military; seeking a career in business.

ABEL BAKER

127 Hampton Street
Rockville, MD 20850

Residence: (301) 555-3784
Answering Service: (301) 555-4895

QUALIFICATIONS AND OBJECTIVES

Rising from staff sergeant to the rank of captain is a clear indication of reliability, leadership, and character. Ten years of highly successful logistics management have prepared me to manage the transportation/trucking division of a medium-sized organization in need of cost efficiency and innovation.

> POSITIVE AND CONVINCING

WORK EXPERIENCE

- Organized, managed, and budgeted for a 140-vehicle transportation center with an annual operating budget of nearly $1 million.

- Initiated, developed, and directed a computer scheduling system that resulted in a 25% improvement of deliveries and an annual cost savings of $209,000.

> COST SAVINGS

- Created and implemented a revised bidding system on all vehicles purchased, allowing for quicker purchase decisions and increased opportunity for price reductions to multiple purchases.

> EFFICIENCY

- Effectively implemented personnel policies that led to a 19% increased efficiency rating over a two-year period. Received two commendations from management leadership.

- Improved measurement and communication of safety-related issues, resulting in nineteen months of accident-free work activity (one month short of the all-time division record).

> CONCISE, BALANCED, COMPREHENSIVE STATEMENTS

WORK HISTORY

1988 - Present: Regional Director, Transportation and Logistics Command, U.S. Army, Washington, D.C.
1982 - 1988: Director, Transportation Section, Fort Campbell, Georgia
1978 - 1982: Division Manager, Motor Pool, Fort Campbell, Georgia
1976 - 1978: Supply Officer, 3rd Army, Stuttgart, Germany

> PROMOTED THROUGH THE RANKS

MILITARY RANK
Captain, U.S. Army

> ALWAYS LIST SUCCESSFUL MILITARY ACHIEVEMENTS

EDUCATION

Diploma, Greensboro High School, Greensboro, North Carolina

FOREIGN LANGUAGES
Spanish, Vietnamese

> EMPHASIZES SKILLS AND EXPERIENCE THAT ARE OF INTEREST TO POTENTIAL EMPLOYERS; DE-EMPHASIZES THOSE THAT ARE LESS SO

COMBINED

Resume Example #6: A hospital care specialist demonstrates his versatility and broad range of skills.

SHERMAN N. JECTION

1 Maywood Road
Roanoke, VA 24014

Residence: (804) 555-0001
Business: (804) 555-1000

EXPERIENCE

October 1991 to
Present

MEDICAL CARE ASSOCIATES   Asheville, North Carolina
GENERAL MANAGER
Directly responsible for all operations of a Medicare-certified home health care agency with annual revenue of $4,200,000. Major services include home health care, private duty care, and supplemental staffing. Nine hundred full- and part-time employees; five branch offices.

> DEMONSTRATES
> ORIENTATION AND VALUE OF
> MANAGEMENT ACTION

- Reorganized internal operations, resulting in monthly savings of $10,000.
- Implemented marketing programs and internal controls that resulted in 20% increase in sales.
- Managed successful transition from franchise operation to corporate branch.
- Directed implementation of computerized client and employee information system.

March 1986 to
October 1991

WALTER A. CUMMINS HOSPITAL SYSTEM   Mobile, Alabama
DIRECTOR OF MANAGEMENT SERVICES -   November 1987 to October 1991
BEAUMONT SHARED SERVICES, INC.
Responsible for several major components of $30,000,000 per year for-profit subsidiary of hospital. Responsibilities included contract management, management consulting, strategic planning, business development, and home health care.

- Planned and implemented establishment of durable medical equipment subsidiary; generated over $400,000 in revenue. $40,000 in profit during first year.
- Initiated first comprehensive strategic planning process for Cummins Shared Services.

> HAS AN EYE FOR EARNINGS

- Expanded contract management to include four hospitals and various consulting projects; generated revenue in excess of $200,000 per year.
- Designed comprehensive wage and benefit program for Shared Services employees; reduced personnel expenses by 15%, but maintained current staffing levels.
- Invited to speak as guest lecturer for Alabama Hospital Association on hospitals and home health care.

CHRONOLOGICAL

SHERMAN N. JECTION
Page 2

ASSISTANT DIRECTOR   *March 1986 to October 1987*

Complete administrative responsibility for patient support departments
of 950-bed teaching hospital. Responsible for 520 employees and annual
budget of $6,600,000.

> VERSATILE AND
> ADVENTURESOME

- Planned and helped initiate conversion of former school into comprehensive outpatient health center.
- Organized and conducted major consulting projects in Nigeria and Saudi Arabia.
- Initiated the planning process required to streamline functions of patient service departments.

September 1984 to   **ARKANSAS COMMUNITY HOSPITAL**   Little Rock, Arkansas
March 1984   *ADMINISTRATOR*
                       *Full responsibility for twenty-five-bed acute care hospital with annual
                       budget of $2,500,000.*

March 1980 to   **NORTH VIRGINIA HOSPITAL SYSTEM**   Arlington, Virginia
March 1986   *ADMINISTRATIVE ASSOCIATE*   *February 1983 to March 1984*
                       *Responsible for management functions of Clinical Pathology
                       Department, which employed 250. Areas of responsibility included:
                       fiscal management, laboratory and employee representation to
                       administration, operational policies and procedures.*

                       PERSONNEL ASSISTANT   *November 1981 to January 1983*
                       *Responsible for provision of personnel services to all areas of hospital.
                       Developed department's data processing systems. Administered wage
                       and salary and grievance programs.*

                       FINANCIAL ANALYST   *March 1980 to October 1981*
                       *Assisted in preparation of revenue, expense, and capital budgets.
                       Prepared and analyzed monthly variance reports and financial
                       statements. Managed hospital's investment portfolio.*

May 1978 to   **WOODWORTH DEPARTMENT STORE**   Washington, D.C.
March 1980   *FINANCIAL ANALYST*

MILITARY   **U.S. ARMY**   *November 1976 to November 1978*
SERVICE: Stationed at Pentagon. Honorable discharge.

EDUCATION: **M.B.A.** **Howard University**   **1982**   **Hospital Administration**
                       M.A.   **Jackson State**   **1980**   **Guidance and Counseling**
                       B.S.   **Morgan State**   **1976**   **Economics and Business
                                                                       Administration**

AFFILIATIONS: *AMERICAN COLLEGE OF HOSPITAL ADMINISTRATORS (member)*

Resume Example #7: *An ex-offender who has changed his ways makes even the worst of his experiences work for him.*

REX CONN

12591 Euclid Avenue
East Cleveland, Ohio 44112

Business: (216) 555-1261

> A DELICATE ISSUE IS WORDED NICELY

CAREER OBJECTIVE: *To apply my extensive firsthand experience in career and crisis counseling of ex-offenders and probationers which helped them strengthen their lives and make positive adjustments to society.*

EXPERIENCE:

COUNSELING: Considerable experience as a result of over 300 one-on-one counseling sessions with ex-offenders in the areas of career assessment and drug and alcohol abuse.

PROGRAM DESIGN: Initiated, designed, and implemented a career/life planning workshop that resulted in nearly 220 probationary attendees participating, with over 50% landing jobs within six months of the program's completion.

LEADERSHIP: Headed up the Prison Reform Board, a sixteen-member state organization designed to improve prison conditions and treatment of inmates.

> SIX ACTION STATEMENTS

HUMAN RELATIONS: Developed reputation in working with diverse ethnic/neighborhood groups to encourage probationary individuals to avail themselves of counseling. Written up in *Cleveland Plain Dealer* as a neighborhood activist.

MANAGEMENT: Lead counselor over nine other counselors in evening crisis intervention center. During fourteen months as lead counselor, center handled over 4,000 phone calls and 1,900 walk-ins.

CITIZENSHIP: Secretary for Cleveland Concerned Citizens, a civic organization dedicated to helping ex-offenders establish productive lives in the community.

> PROFESSIONAL CREDENTIALS

MEMBER OF NATIONAL ASSOCIATION OF CAREER COUNSELORS

EDUCATION:

> IMPORTANT TO INCLUDE

Bachelor of Science Degree, to be obtained June 1996, Cleveland State University
Major in Guidance and Counseling

ADDITIONAL EDUCATION: Crisis intervention workshop, through Ohio Guidance and Counseling Association, 1988; seminar entitled "Alcohol and Substance Abuse," sponsored by Cleveland Chapter of National Association of Career Counselors, 1990.

> VITAL UNDER THESE CIRCUMSTANCES

REFERENCES: Outstanding references available on request.

> TRANSFORMS AN UNFORTUNATE EXPERIENCE INTO A POSITIVE AND OPTIMISTIC CAREER

FUNCTIONAL

Resume Example #8: *An administrator planning a career change.*

ELLEN McSELLWELL

310 El Camino Road
San Diego, California 92103

Residence: (619)555-0000
Business: (619)555-0001

OBJECTIVE   HOSPITAL AND MEDICAL SALES REQUIRING EXTENSIVE EXPERIENCE WITH STATE-OF-THE-ART MEDICAL EQUIPMENT, OUTSTANDING COMMUNICATIONS SKILLS, AND STRONG MOTIVATION.

> PARTICULARLY IMPORTANT TO STATE OBJECTIVE WHEN CHANGING CAREERS

PROFESSIONAL ACCOMPLISHMENTS

> CLEVER STATEMENT

- Successfully conducted training seminars for nearly two hundred supervisory personnel in interpersonal skills.

> COMPETITIVE

- Developed reputation for simultaneously coordinating numerous involved projects. Written up in *Hospital Administrator* magazine, 1990.

- Retained by three directors. Appointed to current position over fourteen other qualified candidates.

- Achievement-motivated, conscientious, objectives-directed. Obtained highest performance rating for three years.

> SALES-ORIENTED

- Adept at problem resolution and public relations. Regularly represent hospital at major civic gatherings.

- Experienced in the development of management systems, including the administration of a $4.3 million budget.

- Active member of Medical Equipment Review Committee, 1991-1994.

- Received U.S. security clearance.

EMPLOYMENT HISTORY

1990 - Present: Administrative Assistant to the Director, San Diego Memorial Hospital

1984 - 1990: Administrator to the Chief of Medical Administration, San Diego

1982 - 1984: Sold LaBelle health and beauty products door-to-door in West Virginia

EDUCATION   B.A., Administrative Management
Marshall University; Huntington, West Virginia

Additional course work at University of San Diego in Group Dynamics, Management, and Psychology

ADDITIONAL EDUCATION

> UTILIZING SKILLS AND ACCOMPLISHMENTS TO CONSTRUCT A NEW CAREER

Job Enrichment	Hospital Supervision
Advance Management	Kepner-Tregoe Problem Solving
AMA Supervisory Skills	T.A. for Supervisors

PERSONAL   Able and willing to relocate and/or travel extensively.

> KEY STATEMENT FOR ANYONE WANTING TO BREAK INTO SALES

COMBINED

Resume Example #9: *A research scientist who isn't looking for a job, at present.*

GINO A. LOGICO

29 Vauxhall Road   Work: (317) 555-1587
Indianapolis, Indiana 46250   Home: (317) 555-9299

EMPLOYMENT HISTORY

■ **WALLACE LABS, INDIANAPOLIS, INDIANA**   **1992 TO PRESENT**

Research Scientist
Research and coordinate development of enzyme immunoassays for diagnostic products. Responsibilities include developing and implementing protein purification procedures, enzyme-antibody conjugates, and solid phase technology for EIAs. Develop scaleup procedures to be used in manufacturing diagnostic products.

> GOOD APPEALING ACTION VERBS

■ **ACADEMIC PRESS, NEW YORK, NEW YORK**   **1986 TO 1992**

Production/Project Editor
Coordinated production of scientific treatises and textbooks from manuscript to bound book. Participated in planning of marketing strategies. Edited and rewrote technical material.

> CLEAR AND EASY TO READ

■ **AMERICAN INSTITUTE OF PHYSICS, NEW YORK, NEW YORK**   **1983 TO 1986**

Production/Project Editor
Controlled production of *Review of Scientific Instruments*, a monthly journal. Rewrote and edited technical manuscripts.

EDUCATION

■ **INDIANA MEDICAL CENTER, INDIANA STATE UNIVERSITY, BLOOMINGTON, INDIANA**

Ph.D. in PHARMACOLOGY   **1987 TO 1992**
Past five years have included extensive laboratory research and experimentation in the following areas:

Drug receptor studies	Drug-induced changes in enzyme activity
Regulation of in-vitro cell proliferation	Protein biochemistry
HPLC (attended seminar course)	Enzyme purification

■ **UNIVERSITY OF ILLINOIS (DOWNSTATE), URBANA, ILLINOIS**

B.S. in BIOLOGY   **1979 TO 1983**
Graduated summa cum laude; 3.81 cumulative index. Elected to several honor societies; received Dean's Award for scholastic excellence.

> WORTH MENTIONING

CHRONOLOGICAL

GINO A. LOGICO
Page 2

PUBLICATIONS   IMPORTANT FOR A RESEARCHER

- March 1994: *Biochemical Pharmacology* (Vol.34, No.6, pp. 811-819). Title: Effect of Streptozotocin on the Glutathione S-transfers of mouse liver cytosol.
- August 1993: *Journal of Laboratory and Clinical Medicine* (Vol.100, No.2, pp. 178-185). Title: Identification of a glucocorticoid receptor in the human leukemia cell line K562.
- November 1992: *Blood* (Vol.58, No.5, Suppl. 1, p. 120(a)). Abstract: same title as article above.

RELATED ACTIVITIES

Downstate, University of Indiana: Instruction of medical students in pharmacology. Tutored undergraduate students in science and mathematics.

SPECIAL SKILLS

NICE ADDITION

Computer literate

PERSONAL DATA   UNNECESSARY, BUT CAN'T HURT

Married, two children

Resume Example #10: A graphic design professional tracks his progression into management.

MICHAEL ANGELO

3000 S. Valley View Blvd.   (702) 555-9999
Las Vegas, Nevada 89102

OBJECTIVE   *Management position in visual communications where strong operations management, graphic design capacity, and ability to develop staff will contribute to the productivity and profitability of the organization.*

> WELL-STATED OBJECTIVE

PROFESSIONAL SUMMARY   *Versatile graphic design professional with thirty years of marketing-oriented experience including production management, two- and three-dimensional graphic problem solving, staff development, logistic sensitivity, in-depth knowledge of reproduction systems, and long-standing record in creative resolution of customer needs.*

> OBJECTIVE SUMMARY BACKED BY DETAILS THAT FOLLOW

SIGNIFICANT ACCOMPLISHMENTS

> SPECIFIC MEASURABLE ACCOMPLISHMENTS

MANAGEMENT, OPERATIONS

- Restructured production organization of 190 employees with fifteen supervisors on three shifts to 170 employees with eleven supervisors on two shifts while accommodating 20% increase in sales and workload.
- Streamlined procedures integrating related creative functions under fewer supervisors. Created multi-skilled technicians to avoid overstaffing. Annual profit increased from $65,000 to $750,000 in two years.
- Reversed operating losses in group producing $360,000 in annual sales. Increased group sales to $1,365,000. Workforce reduced from eleven to eight; group is now a profit leader.
- Authored purchasing/receiving/inventory control program to reduce inventory on hand by 50%, to $225,000. Upgraded requisition system from numbered adhesive tags to electronic entry. Revision allowed first accurate P&L reports.

MANAGEMENT, HUMAN RESOURCES

- Instituted revolutionary employee evaluation procedure to include employee in performance analysis, goal setting, and determination of wage adjustment. Ninety-five percent of employees rated themselves more critically (and requested smaller wage increases) than under previous system.
- Eliminated historic animosity between first and second shift personnel through structured team activity and promotion concept of "sixteen-hour work cycle" to replace existing attitudes of two competing shifts.
- Identified critical system failure—order writers not trained in production methods and capabilities. Over 20% of orders impossible to complete as written. Instituted scheduled training program; erroneous orders still declining.

COMBINED

MICHAEL ANGELO
Page 2

CREATIVE PROBLEM SOLVING

- Conceived, developed, and produced photographically generated color sample booklets to resolve client frustrations when specifying photographic color from process ink samples in standard PMS color swatch books.
- Produced 12-foot-high black and white mural from vertical crop of 16mm movie frame; heavily retouched intermediate 20" x24" print. Copy negative of retouched print produced mural in three sections through fine mezzotint screen. Mural still on display.
- Provided display text in Arabic, German, and Russian using New York-based translation services and foreign-language typesetters. Obtained necessary entry permits and approvals; produced export documents. Arranged pre-paid services.
- Produced full-color mural to be self-supporting in traveling use as backdrop for mall fashion shows. Mural in sections, plus supporting devices, fit into carrying case less than 36" x 36".

PROGRAM DESIGN

- Consulted with over two hundred varied clients in need of A/V programs of all types, sizes, and budgets. Advised appropriate use of overhead transparencies vs. 35mm, computer, or optical slices; guided style and format selection. Produced roughs or storyboards from scripts or notes.
- Restructured production system and quotation to produce environmental graphics for client hospital when original quote of $400,000 proved beyond budget tolerance. Project completed for $160,000.
- Managed graphic production of major space museum project at Jackson Community College. Schedule allowed six weeks from receipt of text, NASA transparencies, and artifacts to opening. Installation completed prior to opening.

EMPLOYMENT HISTORY

1989 - Present	WONDERFULLY CREATIVE	Director of Production
1984 - 1989	GRAPHIC DESIGNS, INC.	Manager, Design and Display
1980 - 1984	SOMEWHAT CREATIVE DESIGNS, LTD.	Graphics Manager
		Director Of Show Services
1974 - 1980	DETROIT EDISON COMPANY	Export Manager
	GRAPHIC DESIGNER	Account Representative

MANAGEMENT DEVELOPMENT PROGRAMS

Statistical Process Control—Oakland University
The Deming Method—George Washington University
Investment in Excellence—Pacific Institute
Effective Team Facilitation—J. Farr
American Economic System—Oakland University
Managing Stress—R. Goren
Communicating for Action—T. Stafford
Statistical Thought Process—Beta Association

EDUCATION   Advertising Design—Center for Creative Studies

Resume Example #11: A middle-aged executive looking for a top management spot.

11 Cordial Avenue
Ridgefield Park, New Jersey 07660

Home (201) 555-9876
Office (201) 555-0001

NOAH A. LOTTS

| OBJECTIVE: | Senior Corporate Planner, General Manager, or Chief Marketing Officer |

DIVISIONAL VICE PRESIDENT

PULLING ALL THE ELEMENTS TOGETHER: IMPACT, SKILLS, ACCOUNTABILITY, EXPERIENCE, SUCCESS

Profit and loss responsibility for corporation with annual sales volume of $76 million. Corporation acquired by growing conglomerate resulting in restructured sales organization, leading to expanded market reach. Developed new market strategy, added new sales representatives, dropped two unprofitable products and added three new products. Strategy allowed for 21% sales increase and profit increase of $3.7 million.

MARKETING, PRODUCTION, AND GENERAL MANAGEMENT

IT WOULD BE DIFFICULT TO FORMULATE MORE IMPRESSIVE ACCOMPLISHMENTS THAN THESE

- *Initiated* and *managed* design and implementation of new product line with eventual sales record of $12.7 million over first two years.
- *Developed* and *implemented* three-year plan to upgrade efficiency of extensive line operation including a capital expenditure commitment of $9.3 million.
- *Decreased* $900,000 accounts receivable collections from 87-day average to less than 35 days.
- *Initiated* improving scheduling system resulting in reduction of delivery time by half.

VICE PRESIDENT CORPORATE PLANNING

INNOVATIVE

- *Introduced* "Results Oriented Management" (MBO) approach to $750 million insurance company that led to a bottom line increase of 29% during a down economy.
- *Developed* and *implemented* $310 million acquisition program over five-year period utilizing stock/tax advantages leading to R.O.I improvement of 19%.
- *Created* product development group, which delivered six new insurance programs over three-year period leading to sales of $19 million and profit of $31 million.

CHIEF MARKETING OFFICER

PROBLEM SOLVING

- *Conceived* of and *marketed* credit card program leading to $131 million in gross revenues over four-year period.
- *Developed* award-winning advertising program with annual budget of $9 million.
- *Revamped* product line that suffered loss of 15% in market share, resulting in recapture of 27% of market over three-and-a-half-year period.
- *Reorganized* forty-seven-member sales organization, allowing for increased field time and reduced travel, and resulting in a decrease in sales expenditures of $1.5 million in one year.

COMBINED

NOAH A. LOTTS
Page 2

EMPLOYMENT HISTORY			
	1989 - PRESENT	Executive Vice President Sales & Marketing	Cubic Systems Bloomfield, New Jersey
	1983 - 1989	Vice President Corporate Planning	Quadrangle International, Hoboken, New Jersey
SOLID	1974 - 1983	Sales Manager	Gotham Insurance, Inc. Wilmington, Delaware
	1966 - 1974	Loan Officer	Metal Specialties Corp., Syracuse, New York
	1963 - 1966	Bank Teller	First National Bank, Hartford, Connecticut
MILITARY SERVICE	1961 - 1963	1st Lieutenant, Communications	U.S. Army
EDUCATION	1960	Bachelor of Arts Business Administration	New York University
FOREIGN LANGUAGES	Spanish, Portuguese, French		

TELLING WHAT YOU'VE DONE
WITH DIGNITY . . . WHEN
THERE IS A GOOD DEAL TO
TALK ABOUT

Resume Example #12: An engineer with well-chosen accomplishment statements and a marketing flair.

JULIO IGLESIAS GARCIA

1001 ASUNCION
SAN JUAN, PR 00920

TEL.: 807/555-2333

EMPLOYMENT 1990 to PRESENT	**Carib Electro Corporation,** San Juan—Service and Quality Control Manager. Responsible for field and customer service activities along with quality control inspection of equipment to insure compliance with customer, OSHA, and JIC standards. Additional responsibilities include purchasing and technical service manual writing.

ATTENTION: PROSPECTIVE EMPLOYERS

- Organized six-person service department to perform SAE certification testing verification of systems, resulting in 60% increase in contract revenues, along with warranty and non-warranty repairs leading to a 45% increase in repeat sales.
- Wrote technical operation and maintenance manuals for all systems manufactured.
- Reduced purchasing costs by 32% by developing and utilizing purchasing program for TRS80 computer.

BOTTOM-LINE ORIENTED

1984 to 1990

ABZ Corporation, Xeroradiography Division—Technical Specialist. Responsible for field service and support of all technical representatives and contractors within designated region.

- *Promoted* from technical representative in Ponce branch to specialist within nine months of employment; became responsible for San Juan territory.
- *Reduced* nationwide service call rate by developing and implementing various in-field system retrofits.
- *Relocated* to develop new area in Denver-based territory, resulting in area sales increase of thirty-five systems the following year.

GETS RESULTS

EDUCATION

DRAWS OUT BUSINESS AND HUMAN BEHAVIOR CLASSES

New York University, November 1984—Bachelor of Applied Science, Electronic Engineering Technology. Graduated with 3.95/4.0 GPA; primary concentrations in business communication, personnel administration, human resource management, business law, principles of marketing, and behavioral psychology.

RETS Electronic, June 1982—Associate's Degree in Electronic Engineering Technology. Second Class FCC Radio Telephone license.

ACTIVITIES

Participating member of Society of Technical Communication (STC).

SPECIAL SKILLS

Bilingual (English/Spanish)

ESSENTIAL FOR THIS LOCATION

CHRONOLOGICAL

Resume Example #13: A mid-level manager looking to make a substantial jump in responsibility.

ERIC VON HOHAUSER

79 Brampton Street
Bismarck, North Dakota 58010

Residence: 701/555-1001
Business: 701/555-0110

PROFESSIONAL EXPERIENCE: Twenty years of administrative and sales management in finance and insurance. Consistent record of improving financial results, operational effectiveness, and customer service.

As *Financial Services Manager* for LIFE ENHANCE INSURANCE CO., was responsible on a national basis for new account installations, new business development, and marketing of financial products. Conducted seminar presentations to potential customer groups on a variety of financial topics relating to our product capabilities. Extremely knowledgeable concerning all phases of consumer lending regulations. Headed up project and marketed microcomputer system that has been installed in over three hundred credit unions. Designed and implemented an IRA product that has been sold to over one hundred credit unions in first six months. 1991 - Current

> HIGHLIGHTS SALES AND PRODUCT MANAGEMENT CAPABILITIES

While at LAUREL SCHOOLS CREDIT UNION, was Operations Officer directly responsible for internal operations of this $22 million financial institution with thirty-three employees. Was *Chief Operating Officer*; personally administered all lending activities, accounting, staff training, loan delinquencies, and work flow scheduling. Implemented revolving credit loan system. Designed marketing promotions and more efficient services resulting in assets increasing from $10 million to $22 million in two years. 1985-1991

> POINTS OUT GENERAL
> MANAGEMENT EXPERIENCE

While at MANUFACTURERS BANK, originated and handled underwriting for short-term commercial construction loans; supervised $22 million portfolio. Designed operating procedures for branch office and main office departments. Developed procedures for implementation of Master Charge system, conducted training sessions with over three hundred branch personnel. Conducted analysis resulting in purchase and installation of such equipment as high-speed check photographing machines, branch camera equipment, and teller machines. 1980-1985

> GOOD PARAGRAPHS THAT COVER A VARIETY OF ADMINISTRATIVE TALENTS

Began as *Management Trainee* at HAYDEN & RUIZ. Quickly looped through all sales, administration, and operations groups in 18 months; was selected to fill new operations position responsible for identifying and acting on all work flow opportunities. In three and a half years in this position was able to significantly impact speed of customer service and quality of information/data available to staff to make decisions. Also reduced operating expenses. 1975-1980

COMMUNITY ACTIVITIES:

Chairman, Administrative committee for St. Michael's Parish.
Member, Citizens Advisory Group for Board of Education.

> EACH OF THE FOUR PARAGRAPHS
> ILLUSTRATES A SET OF SKILLS THAT
> HIGHLIGHT THIS INDIVIDUAL'S
> VERSATILITY

EDUCATION:

B.B.A. - University of Miami, Business Administration.

CHRONOLOGICAL

Resume Example #14: A senior-level executive who effectively highlights her successes in the international arena.

CONSTANCE WORLDLY

1696 SOUTH FOURTH STREET   RESIDENCE: (215)321-2121
PHILADELPHIA, PENNSYLVANIA 19147   MESSAGES: (215)321-3232

> MODESTLY STATED

OBJECTIVE

Resourceful, results-oriented executive accustomed to profit and loss responsibilities seeks domestic or international marketing position, preferably in high-tech materials manufacturing.

BACKGROUND SUMMARY

> COMPREHENSIVE SUMMARY

Extensive experience principally at executive level in international and domestic marketing, manufacturing, and engineering research and development, for $115 million manufacturer of precision specialty metal products. Strengths in development of production facilities and licensees in Europe and the Far East. Distinguished record in new product development and patents. Solid background in managing start-up and ongoing production operations.

> ACTION PHRASES SUPPORT
> OBJECTIVE AND SUMMARY

CAREER HISTORY

MONOLITHIC INDUSTRIES, Philadelphia, Pennsylvania   1981 - PRESENT
VICE PRESIDENT, INTERNATIONAL OPERATIONS: 1992 - PRESENT
Direct overseas marketing and licensees in Europe and Asia for manufacturer of bearings and friction materials. Annual revenue from licensees up to $25 million.

- Instructed Japanese licensee on bearing manufacturing processes including powder-making, strip sintering, and related operations. Increased license fees by 315% per year.
- Designed and arranged financing for $16 million bearings manufacturing plant in India, generating a $5.5 million profit on $14 million in equipment sales.
- Researched market, established process, and designed manufacturing facility for low-cost production of cam bushings in mainland China for $37 million worldwide market.

GENERAL MANAGER, BEARINGS DIVISION: 1989 - 1992

> MEASURABLE RESULTS

Profit and loss responsibility for all operations, including manufacturing, quality, engineering, finance, personnel, and marketing. Annual sales $60 million. Staff of eight hundred in four facilities.

- Restructured division on a product-line basis generating an additional 8% gross margin, reducing inventory $3 million, and increasing profits by $2.5 million from a loss position in first year of operation.
- Directed start-up of production at 100,000 square foot manufacturing plant.
- Increased market share to 60% at three major automobile companies in a declining market.

CHRONOLOGICAL

Resume Example #14 continued.

CONSTANCE WORLDLY
Page 2

PROGRESSION OF
RESPONSIBILITIES

DIRECTOR OF SALES AND MARKETING: 1984 - 1988
Directed marketing program for OEM bearings and transmission parts. Annual sales: $75 million.
- Organized and staffed complete marketing activity. Sales growth compounded at 17% per year ($10 to $40 million) in nine years; non-automotive sales increased 300%.
- Established European licensees resulting in a $9.5 million equipment order in Rumania, licensees in France and Germany, plus new major customer accounts.

DIRECTOR OF RESEARCH AND DEVELOPMENT: 1981 - 1984
Directed materials research, process development, and customer engineering activities.
- Developed unique asbestos-free, paper-based friction materials generating $15 million sales (60% gross profit).
- Analyzed process for sintering of copper-lead on steel strip yielding a 300% increase in output and 40% cost reduction for a $11 million annual savings.

ALLOYS, INCORPORATED; JENNINGS, IOWA   [MORE THAN TEN YEARS PAST, BUT SHOWS SOLID TECHNICAL BACKGROUND]   1975 - 1981
RESEARCH METALLURGIST
Studied wear and fatigue properties of metals. Developed new materials involving the sintering and casting of non-ferrous metals.

EDUCATION
University of Nebraska - B.S., Physics and Mathematics
Advanced Management Training courses on Manufacturing Strategy at Harvard University Business School and at Iowa State University Graduate School of Sales and Marketing.

PATENTS AND PUBLICATIONS
Twenty-one patents dealing with materials and processes.
Numerous articles in a variety of technical and marketing publications.

[A PROSPECTIVE EMPLOYER WILL WANT TO KNOW THE DETAILS IN AN INTERVIEW]

ASSOCIATIONS
Society of Automotive Engineers - American Society for Metals.

Resume Example #15: A credit manager highlights his creativity and proven ability to create new business.

ADAM SMITH

19008 Holparken Square
Des Moines, Iowa 50336

Residence: (515) 555-0001
Business: (515) 555-0002

AN EFFECTIVE ALTERNATIVE
TO THE CAREER OBJECTIVE:
CALLS ATTENTION TO
SKILLS, CAPABILITIES, AND
INDUSTRY EXPERIENCE

ADMINISTRATION and MARKETING
CREDIT MANAGEMENT ... PRODUCT PROMOTION
HOUSING ... RECREATIONAL PRODUCTS ... EXPORTING

An entrepreneurial manager with a strong credit background who has worked closely with company marketing personnel in setting up a solid dealer organization. Record of working cross-functionally with sales, marketing, operations, manufacturing, and customer service to identify and realize opportunities to enhance products and product sales. Experienced in working with federal and state agencies and top management to adapt and promote the company's products.

SIGNIFICANT ACCOMPLISHMENTS

CREDIT MANAGEMENT
- Implemented "private brands" finance program with vice president of marketing to make program more understandable and to speed up paperwork process.
- Prevented potential loss of $110,000 by moving quickly and securing debtor's business property to insure debt payment.
- Served on finance committee of Manufactured Housing Institute for several years; coordinated activities with federal agencies (HUD, FHA, and VA) on housing matters.
- Testified for company at twelve trials involving legal and bankruptcy proceedings against former accounts.
- Knowledgeable in Uniform Commercial Code and all necessary filings required to protect company's security interest in inventory.

THESE SUPPORT "CAREER"
HEADING AND PROVIDE
INTERNAL INTEGRITY

MARKETING
- Promoted company's product lines through European trade office of State of Iowa by providing literature and quotations to interested foreign firms. Six requests for proposals resulted.
- Initiated concept and promoted "Ways to Be a Successful Dealer" to four hundred mobile home dealers at national mobile home show seminar.
- Instrumental in selling $650,000 of repossessed inventory of specially built tractor-trailer equipment at no loss to employer.
- Established land-home sales program for dealers in southeastern United States with national finance company, resulting in over $500,000 in additional business.

COMBINED

ADAM SMITH
Page 2

CREATIVE PROGRAMS

- Generated additional sales and profits by inviting trade specialist for U.S. Department of Commerce to advise top management on promoting products overseas.
- Persuaded Builders Credit to perform additional credit investigation program on new dealer applicants in order to reduce future losses.
- Initiated credit interchange program with twelve other credit managers within industry to identify problem accounts and reduce potential losses.
- Developed (with top management and U S. Department of Commerce's Jamaican office) moderately priced housing units to meet housing needs of hurricane-devastated Jamaica.

SUPPORTS HEADING AND
SHOWS VERSATILITY

EMPLOYMENT HISTORY

1986 - Present	Labor Division Home Builders Co.	CREDIT MANAGER
1981 - 1986	Nations Wealth National Bank	ASSISTANT CREDIT MANAGER
1975 - 1981	Laissez-Faire, Inc.	SALES AND LEASING REPRESENTATIVE

EDUCATION

B. S. Finance - University of Scotland, 1970
Completed 10 credits toward M.B.A. at University of Detroit, 1974 - 75

Resume Example #16: An upbeat, creative presentation of an impressive track record in big-ticket marketing.

Merrie R. Noël
200 Nesbit Trail
Alpharetta, Georgia 30201
(404)555-0000

OBJECTIVE   Endless horizons in marketing or sales management with a progressive, dynamic company that needs and appreciates a results-oriented and highly experienced professional.

PROFESSIONAL ACHIEVEMENTS

STRATEGIC ACCOUNT MANAGER
- Achieved superior track record in developing new business.
- Implemented new market strategies to establish added value programs resulting in $17 million of new business over a two-year period.
- Researched and analyzed market trends in specific consumer and industrial market segments to ensure fitness of products for growth.

RESULTS THAT COUNT

SENIOR FIELD MARKET DEVELOPMENT SPECIALIST
- Identified and developed over $10 million of new business.
- Developed successful partnerships with strategic end user companies.
- Positioned new materials for developing applications providing manufacturing advantages to the end user.

LONG- AND SHORT-TERM SUCCESSES

- Integrated resources into end user engineering and design functions to optimize material selection, performance, and design for manufacturability.
- Coordinated product, molding, and design seminars resulting in joint development programs with end user companies.

VICE PRESIDENT

ENTREPRENEURSHIP

- Co-founded First Source Corporation, a manufacturer and distributor of specialty and proprietary chemicals for the food, pharmaceutical, and personal care industries.
- Nurtured this entrepreneurial venture from infancy into a $3 million business in thirty-six months.
- Maintained responsibility for sales, marketing, profit, and loss.

PRODUCT MANAGER, SILICONE FLUIDS   MORE SOLID RESULTS
- Developed and implemented marketing strategies for nationally marketed silicones.
- Increased sales volumes from $7 million to $12 million by second year.
- Motivated, directed, and routed activities of seven sales representatives and twenty-two distributors.
- Designed, coordinated, and implemented a professional/educational training program for corporate and distributor sales forces.

COMBINED

Merrie R. Noël
Page 2

SALES REPRESENTATIVE, INORGANIC CHEMICALS
- Conducted extensive market research project on fire extinguishing agent. Study resulted in $2 million gross sales within eleven months of completion.
- Increased department's sales from $10 million to $13 million after twelve months.

ASSISTANT TO DIRECTOR OF MARKETING
- Coordinated product evaluations/approvals with major U.S. customers for the eight products sold to U.S. licensees abroad.
- Conducted extensive market research projects to assist in developing product strategies for U.S. market.

BUYER, IMPORT PURCHASING
- Directly responsible for purchasing $75 million of products (raw material ingredients and imported resale items).

EMPLOYMENT HISTORY

HF PLASTICS, Pittsfield, Massachusetts	**1986 TO Present**
STRATEGIC ACCOUNT MANAGER	1988 - Present
SENIOR FIELD MARKET DEVELOPMENT SPECIALIST	1987 - 1988
FIELD MARKET DEVELOPMENT SPECIALIST	1986 - 1987
FIRST SOURCE CORPORATION, Cedar Hills, Illinois	**1983 TO 1986**
VICE PRESIDENT	1983 - 1986
POUNE-ROLANC, INC., Tillamook Junction, New Jersey	**1976 TO 1983**
PRODUCT MANAGER, SILICONE FLUIDS	1982 - 1983
SALES REPRESENTATIVE, INORGANIC CHEMICALS	1980 - 1982
ASSISTANT TO DIRECTOR OF MARKETING, ORGANIC CHEMICALS	1978 - 1980
BUYER, IMPORT PURCHASING	1976 - 1978

EDUCATION

B.A.–Education, French: University of Delaware, 1974

Management Seminars: American Management Association: 1989
Industrial Market Research: 1987
Purchasing: 1987

Communispond: Effective Presentations; 1988

HF Plastics Management Development Institute

Modern Marketing Course: 1988
Product Planning Course: 1989

SHOWS WILLINGNESS TO
KEEP ON LEARNING

AWARDS

HF Plastics Marketing Division Award—1987
HF Plastics Marketing Division Award—1988

Resume Example #17: A high-level executive who gets it all onto a single page.

ROGER M.B. AIMAN

14 McCaul Street
Toronto, Ontario MST 1WI

Home (416) 555-1514
Office (416) 555-8285

Professional Experience

1988-Present

PUBLISHERS ASSOCIATED SERVICES, INC., Toronto, Ontario
President and Principal - Promote and furnish cost-efficient microcomputer systems to publishing companies. Assist in selection of appropriate hardware and software designed to save time and control costs. Increase editorial and marketing productivity.

> HE SAYS A LOT WITH A FEW WELL-CHOSEN WORDS

1985-1988

> WHEN YOU HAVE ACCOMPLISHED THIS MUCH, DETAILS CAN BE SAFELY SUMMARIZED

THOMAS PUBLICATIONS, Toronto, Ontario
President and CEO - Chief executive in charge of operations for a leading vocational/technical textbook publisher. Exercised P&L authority for all phases of management, including editorial, production, and marketing, with seventy employees reporting.

Executive Vice-President: Reporting to the Chairman of the Board Administered daily operations of Mardel Publishers in Albany, NY. Position combined general management authority with supervision of marketing and sales staff. Established computerized sales information systems, resulting in better allocation of sales territories and improvements in capital investment in publishing projects.

Director, Marketing and Sales: Directed all marketing activities, including advertising, direct mail promotion, product releases, exhibits, and field selling. Developed computer database of mailing list, and organized sales communication system for timely reportage by field sales representatives.

1982-1985

O'BRIEN-HULL BOOK COMPANY OF CANADA, Toronto, Ontario
Held key positions in marketing and sales administration with three text-book divisions: Goutt, Collegiate Community, and Vocational/ Technical. Achievements include development of first integrated product information system for college and technical/vocational ties. Introduced Professional Selling Skills program to college travelers; designed and published Technical Education News quarterly magazine; instrumental in converting catalogs to computer database for electronic typesetting.

Education

1982—M.B.A., University of Toronto Graduate School of Business Administration
1980—B.A., McGill University, Montreal

CHRONOLOGICAL

Resume Example #18: *A recent college graduate who makes an excellent representation of her brief but relevant work experience.*

BEVERLY BARLEYCORN
147 Deerwood Lane
Cedar Rapids, IA 52404
(309) 555-0001

OBJECTIVE

A position in financial administration, financial analysis, financial planning, or funds management that will require my best efforts.

EDUCATION

B.A., Financial Administration, June 1995
Iowa State University
GPA: 3.5/4.0

PROFESSIONAL EMPLOYMENT

Summers 1993 and 1994: Holt Corp., Alpha Insulation Division, Iowa City

- *Financial Analyst:* Analyzed operating, pricing, and purchasing variances weekly. Prepared financial performance reports. Provided financial analysis for special projects. Took part in year-end closing and LIFO cost calculations. Attended budget and forecasting meetings with senior management. Interacted in various controllership duties.

> **THREE WELL-WRITTEN STATEMENTS DEMONSTRATING A BROAD RANGE OF EXPERIENCES**

- *Inventory Control:* Planned and conducted verification systems for the Direct Salesforce to report status of inventories accurately. Audited and reconciled inventories of the vans, mini-warehouses, and regional warehouses. Recommended methods to reduce inventory shrinkage.
- *Credit Analyst:* Responsible for USA Direct Sell operations. Approved or rejected sales orders from customers. Reviewed and revised customer credit limits. Wrote eighty-page procedure manual for the Credit Department to help establish a consistent credit policy. Negotiated special rates with the collection agencies.

POSITIONS HELD WHILE ATTENDING COLLEGE

1991-1995 (part-time): Iowa State University Library
Student Assistant: Duties included processing journals, checking out assigned reading and general books, door checking, and shelving books.

> **WELL-PHRASED STATEMENTS THAT MAKE THE MOST OUT OF EACH POSITION**

1992 (summer): March Companies, Inc., Iowa City
Route Driver: Vacation relief driver; also filled in for terminated salespeople. Responsibilities included selling, delivering, accounting, banking, inventory control, and customer services.

COMBINED

1991 (summer): Karmond Lumber Co., Cedar Rapids
Customer Service: Assisted customers in filling their orders, trained new employees, stocked merchandise, took inventories, and made deliveries to customers' homes.

1990 (summer): Cambridge Condominiums, Cedar Rapids
Maintenance Person: Duties included landscaping and general maintenance.

HONORS AND ACTIVITIES
Dean's Honor List - seven terms
Volunteer Income Tax Assistance
Iowa State Finance Club Membership Director
Gamma Phi Nu Fraternity
Intrafraternity Council Representative

DEMONSTRATES
LEADERSHIP AND
ACHIEVEMENT MOTIVATION

A WELL THOUGHT-OUT
RESUME THAT MAKES
MAXIMUM USE OF THIS
INDIVIDUAL'S OFFERINGS

Resume Example #19: *A highly experienced, versatile, professional manager who puts his best foot forward.*

CHRISTOPHER LIBIDOS

42 East 73rd Avenue
Tulsa, OK 74115

Home: 405/555-0000
Office: 405/555-0001

ABILITY TO IDENTIFY, FORMULATE, AND MARKET HIGH PAYOFF PROJECTS: Developed projects that led to birth of 6,000-terminal communications network and $20 million-a-year wholesale company (the Arbor House Specials seen on TV). Installed M.B.O., and annual marketing plan in division of 1450, and an accounting system for bookstores.

> **WELL-PHRASED HEADINGS**

ABILITY TO START, GROW, AND MANAGE DEPARTMENTS: Started and managed: five training departments, research department, personnel department, and district sales office. Played key role starting seventy national account sales departments and two research departments.

P&L RESPONSIBILITY: Started division with $66,500 budget; now over $2.8 million.

ABILITY TO WORK AT TOP LEVELS: Set up board summit meetings to develop corporate objectives. Directly responsible to board for several projects. Staff person in charge of several board committees. Sold and serviced group coverage working with top management and unions of major companies. Three years as Management Consultant.

SCOPE OF TRAINING EXPERIENCE: Managing and conducting sales training, management and organizational development, and clerical and technical training. Developing. staffing, and selling fifty workshops with 5,000 enrollees per year, throughout North America, on financial and marketing management. Producer of workbooks, movies, programmed instruction, and video programs.

SCOPE OF RESEARCH EXPERIENCE: Managing market research, new product development, operations improvement, R&D, and fact-based development and maintenance. Creating and conducting census of retail flower shops; primary source of data for floral industry.

> **COMBINATION OF EXPERIENCES SHOWS BOTH VERSATILITY AND DEPTH**

POSITIONS:

1991 - Present	Director, Education and Research Division, Arbor House International association; 1200 retail bookstores
1988 - 1991	Management Consultant for consulting firm of Martell and Coxwell, Inc. Worked with National Association of Healthcare Affiliates, Timon Mufflers, and Oceanic Airlines
1986 - 1988	Manager, Employee Development Department, Ohio Healthcare Affiliates
1981 - 1986	Manager of various sales, training, and personnel functions, including the Automobile Club of Ohio

EDUCATION:

B.A., Economics, Washington State University, Seattle, Washington
Over 1500 classroom hours at University of Tulsa, University of Chicago and Ohio State University
RE: Management, Mathematics, Organizational Development, Behavioral Science, and Educational Technology

> **EMPHASIS HERE IS ON CONTINUING EDUCATION**

> **HERE'S ADDITIONAL PROOF THAT A ONE-PAGE RESUME CAN PROVIDE IMPACT**

COMBINED

Resume Example #20: Transforming "housewifery" into job-related skills.

Latta Toffer
327 Carmichael Avenue
Topeka, Kansas 66601
(913) 555-0000

Objective

A challenging position that will both utilize and strengthen the organizational and motivational skills acquired in over eleven years of diverse, demanding responsibilities.

Experience

Recently completed over 11 years as a suburban homemaker and mother of three children, with success and skill in the following areas:

POSITIVE STATEMENT TRANSLATING WORK AND EXPERIENCE INTO JOB-RELATED SKILLS

- Budgeting - Accountable for the control and disbursement of an annual budget of $59,200.

- Prioritizing - Established schedules, met deadlines, and coordinated diverse tasks.

ACTION VERBS, IMPACT STATEMENTS

- Training and Supervision - Trained, instructed, and directed three junior associates, whose development was under my jurisdiction, in a wide variety of skills (from bicycle riding to writing term papers to managing a paper route).

- Recruitment, Interviewing, and Selection of Personnel - Hired a wide variety of professionals, including electricians, physicians, roofers, decorators, and baby-sitters.

- Purchasing- Analyzed and initiated purchases of low-budget to high-ticket items, including two automobiles, 950 square yards of carpeting, a twenty-four-cubic-foot freezer, swim club memberships, orthodontic and medical services, and six rooms of furniture.

VALIDATES CLAIM TO MANAGEMENT SKILLS

NOTE: All the above was accomplished successfully; during this time, a two-year Associate Degree was completed at Topeka Junior College, with membership on the Dean's list five out of six semesters.

NECESSARY IN THIS CASE

Excellent references available upon request.

NO DATES INCLUDED

EMPHASIZES JOB-RELATED SKILLS AND ACHIEVEMENTS

FUNCTIONAL

Resume Example #21: A legal specialist provides in-depth details.

LEON R. LAWLESS

40 Orchard Avenue
Ogden, UT 84404
(801) 555-1389

> NOTHING FANCY HERE;
> STRAIGHTFORWARD FACTS
> TELL IT ALL

EXPERIENCE

1986 - Present **WEDMAN, GIBBONS, GOLDMAN & MOORE**
(1984 spin-off from Moran, Sullivan, Forrest & Yee)
Ogden, UT   ASSOCIATE ATTORNEY

Conduct all aspects of patent prosecution, including: patentability evaluations and validity opinions; evaluations of disclosure letters; disclosure interviews with inventors and counsel; preparation filing, and prosecution of patent applications relating to: silicon polymer chemistry and embodiments covering hard-coatings; adhesives, non-stick coatings, silicon elastomers; production of hyperpure silicon; epoxy resins and curing agents; fiber resin matrix prepegs and composites; emulsion-based paints and coatings; ultraviolet light screening agents; high-temperature lubricants; thermoplastics; secondary oil recovery and transmission of liquid media; highway construction; refractory composites; and steam generators. Examiner interviews; preparation of appeal briefs; oral argument before the Board of Appeals; preparation and prosecution of reissue applications. Responsible for preparation and prosecution of trademark applications, trademark appeals and oral argument before the TTAB, and trademark oppositions. Responsible for all pretrial aspects of patent and trademark litigations. Prepare confidential disclosure agreements, perform legal research, and prepare legal memoranda.

> TECHNICAL DETAILS LIKE
> THESE ARE REQUIRED FOR
> PROFESSIONS SUCH AS LAW

1983 - 1986 **MORAN, SULLIVAN, FORREST & YEE**
Provo, UT   ASSOCIATE ATTORNEY

Managed major aspects of patent prosecution and appeal, including: evaluation of disclosures; interviews with inventors and counsel; preparation, filing, and prosecution of patent applications relating to silicon hard coatings and vulcanites, treated silica fibers, thermoplastics, wire enamels, and frangible adhesive containers; and patent litigation (including drafting and responding to interrogatories, examination and control of documents and exhibits, organizing depositions, legal research, and drafting legal memoranda).

-continued-

CHRONOLOGICAL

1982 - 1983	**HORVATH, SWEENEY & ARCHER** Salt Lake City, UT	

Conducted project to analyze terms of over twelve thousand license agreements and entertainment contracts, and creation of database allowing completion of same.

1975 - 1980
(summers)

BRIGHAM YOUNG UNIVERSITY, Department of Biochemistry
Lab Assistant

Supervised running of continuous, complex protein separation process; responsible for purifying, assaying, and storing selected enzymes; developed mutant strains of Pseudomonas bacteria; maintained and harvested several bacteria cultures.

EDUCATION   J.D. 1981   **BRIGHAM YOUNG UNIVERSITY**
Equitas (BYLS newspaper) writer,
summer intern in City Council
President's Office

B.A. Biological Sciences   **BRIGHAM YOUNG UNIVERSITY**
B.A. Psychology   Microbiology, Physiological Psychology
1979

ADMISSIONS   United States Patent and Trademark Office
Bar of the State of Utah

MEMBERSHIPS   American Bar Association
Copyright Society of the U.S.A.

RELEVANT AND NECESSARY
TO THE LEGAL PROFESSION

Utah Patent, Trademark, and Copyright Law Association
Utah County Lawyers' Association

Resume Example #22: *A homemaker with some earlier professional experience pulls it all together.*

RAMONA REENTRY

1404 Marlboro
Minneapolis, MN 55401

Work (612) 555-0011
Home (612) 555-1100

STRAIGHTFORWARD JOB
OBJECTIVE

OBJECTIVE: Journalism: Financial/Economics /General News Reporting

**SIGNIFICANT
ACCOMPLISHMENTS**

> CREATES A BUSY, EFFICIENT
> IMPRESSION OF SOMEONE
> WHO GETS THINGS DONE

- Initiated, organized, and successfully led PTA. Sponsored one-year fund drive raising $86,250 (1989).
- Selected to five-member Emment County Scholastic Achievement Board, which distributes $50,000 in college scholarships to underprivileged high school seniors.
- Successfully organized 44-member petitioning group, which led to tax referendum being placed on Emment County election ballot—1994.
- Author of fifty-eight page book *"Making Your Money Grow"* directed at eight to sixteen-year olds. Used in twenty-nine school districts.
- Wrote and co-directed play entitled "Life—A Contact Sport" about interpersonal skills useful for high school-age students.
- Chosen as one of four finalists for "Volunteer Citizen of the Year"—1993.
- Regular contributor to the *National Scholastic Achiever*, a quarterly journal. Have published eleven articles from 1987 to present.

> NOTEWORTHY

EDUCATION

- B.S. - Journalism: University of Chicago, 1987. 3.4/4.0 GPA; graduated "with distinction"
- Post-graduate study: Illinois State University, 1991-1993 Economics and Finance—eight classes at senior undergraduate level. 3.9/4.0 GPA

> DEMONSTRATES
> CONTINUATION OF ACTIVE
> INTERESTS

**PROFESSIONAL
EXPERIENCE:**

NATIONAL SCHOLASTIC ACHIEVER   **1993 - Present**
Part-time (twenty hours a week) position—research, writing, and office management.

CHICAGO TRIBUNE   **1987 - 1989**
Special Events Reporter. Left voluntarily to raise family.

> O.K. TO INCLUDE FOR
> SOMEONE NOT CURRENTLY
> EMPLOYED

Excellent references.

COMBINED

Resume Example #23: *A graduating senior with very little work experience searches for his first job.*

RALPH T. RAWFELLOW
212 E. Walnut
Troy, Michigan 48098
(801) 644-1001

EDUCATION

B.S. CANDIDATE, OAKLAND UNIVERSITY, on target for an April 1996 graduation in mechanical engineering.

> **Significant course work in:** Computer Science, Statics, Thermodynamics, Properties of Materials and Electrical Circuitry.
> Overall grade point average (GPA): **3.2/4.0**

SELECTED ACHIEVEMENTS

- Successfully maintained status as co-op student entire senior year of high school, which required satisfactory work performance and GPA.

- Selected for promotion to assistant manager over four colleagues. Responsibilities included leading a staff of subordinates ranging from ten to thirty individuals.

- Received commendation for GPA (3.0 or better) in five of seven semesters at Oakland University.

- Successfully operated plastic injection mold machines producing a variety of products including hydraulic seals. This process entailed machine set-up, operation, and maintenance.

- Recruited to work in child's day care center. Worked ten hours a week for one year. Responsible for the care and supervision of eight children. Consistently recognized by parents with confidence in my ability to care for their children.

- Excellent writing ability as demonstrated by consistently strong grades on English compositions, lab reports, and term papers.

EXPERIENCE

Park Place (Division of Boardwalk, Inc.), Oakland and Fairlane Mall   **May 1993 - present**
Have worked consistently full and part-time as sales clerk and assistant manager, currently as customer service manager. This NYSE company with over four hundred stores has a reputation for training and development of employees. This opportunity has afforded me the chance to face and handle responsibility at a relatively young age. Have maintained a strong work record with Park Place.

Premier Restaurant Services, Inc., Troy, Michigan   **January 1995 - present**
Work on a project basis for this commercial restaurant kitchen installation company. Responsibilities include movement and installation of equipment, construction of shelving units, and assisting in a variety of other jobs as required.

COMBINED

Resume Example #23 continued: This page could be optionally included or excluded.

Grandma Harmon's Day Care, Ferndale, Michigan   September 1992 - September 1993

Recruited by owner of this licensed child care center to position of child supervisor involving the care and protection of eight children ranging in age from two to three years old. Responsibilities included supervision of educational projects and play time.

Target Packing Corporation, Troy, Michigan   **1984 - 1993**

Have worked part-time since the age of eleven. Handled responsibilities ranging from sweeping and cleaning machinery to operating injection molding machinery. The nine years I've worked for Target have allowed me to understand what a business needs to be profitable and to produce quality products.

The Troy Gazette, Troy, Michigan   **1984 - 1988**

Successfully managed paper route with eighty to ninety customers. Awarded trip for signing up twenty new customers. Recognized for good work by receiving "carrier of the week" award.

Resume Example #24: Career enhancement at the middle-management level.

MANLY R. UPBOUND

12 Arcadia Drive
El Paso, Texas 79901

Telephone: (512) 555-6543 (Res.)
(512) 555-1111 (Bus.)

| SPECIFIC AND AMBITIOUS |

CAREER OBJECTIVE: To direct a dynamic, ambitious (small or medium-sized) electronics corporation, and to help it grow into a major industry player.

EMPLOYMENT: 1988 to PRESENT

P. REYNOLDS CORPORATION, El Paso- Texas—*Director of Research and Development. Responsible for new product development and testing from innovation through Feasibility. Includes management of a staff of twenty-three.*

| GOOD BALANCE BETWEEN HISTORY AND ACCOMPLISHMENTS |

- *Recruited* and developed research team of twelve engineers within eighteen months on job. No turnover on staff to date.

| DOLLAR SAVINGS |

- *Developed* methodology of counter redesign of electronic sensing devices. This saved corporation $400,000 in first year of implementation.
- *Managed* R&D team responsible for major design changes to production facility resulting in 30% labor savings.
- *Led* research team that designed and rolled out Lithium Sulfate Battery, which tripled mileage capability of electric automobile.

1981 to 1988

LABORATORY TESTING CORPORATION, Little Rock, Arkansas—*Senior Research Supervisor. Headed up eight-person product testing group responsible for establishing performance specifications.*

| MEASURABLE IMPROVEMENT |

- *Initiated* group performance standards that allowed for "on-time" completion standard of 92%. Prior group had maintained 55% standard.
- *Created* test procedures that revealed product design errors, saving client manufacturers over $2 million during four years in this position.

Research Analyst. Member of a new tooling group developing and testing newly installed manufacturing lines involving high-usage, electronically controlled feeder and assembly units.

- *Supervised* four-person group that blueprinted wiring schematics for entire final production assembly line for Volkswagen of America. Used computer line tracking design of our own making (first time used within automotive industry).

| SHOWS INITIATIVE |

- *Promoted* to group supervisor (youngest supervisor of research group in corporation).

EDUCATION: University of Texas at El Paso, B.S. and M.S.E.E. 1981. Completed graduate work with a 4.8 GPA out of a possible 5.0.

AWARDS: American Society of Electrical Engineers—"Research Engineer of the Year," 1986. Received recognition for usage of voltage conductors in high-use assembly units.

| RELEVANT AWARD |

CHRONOLOGICAL

Resume Example #25: Fast-track creativity seeking career enhancement.

RITA L. FANTASIA

90 Treefilled Lane
Hillsboro, Oregon 97123

Telephone: Home (503) 555-5252
Office (503) 555-2525

EMPLOYMENT:

VENUS BEAUTY PRODUCTS, Portland, Oregon　　　　　　　　1990 - Present
Major beauty products supply distributor and retailer with annual sales of $30 million.
Proprietary Market Manager
Responsibilities:
- Buyer of forty proprietary line items for thirty-eight distribution centers nationwide.
- Annual open to buy budget: $8 million.　　　　　　　**RESPONSIBLE**
- Product and package planning, design, and development.
- Market analysis and research.
- Sales forecasting and evaluation of new and existing products.
- Advertising and promotion including introductory offers and deals, quarterly catalogue, and monthly news articles.

> **UNUSUAL FORMAT SUCCESSFULLY DEMONSTRATES WHAT SHE WAS SUPPOSED TO DO**

Achievements:　　**CREATIVITY**
- Established annual budget for new product development.
- Initiated seven new products from planning to point of purchase within ten months.
- Designed and authored a training manual for sales staff.
- Presented several slide presentations for training sessions.

> **LOOK AT HOW MUCH INFORMATION IS CONTAINED IN ONLY THIRTEEN WORDS**

DEVON INCORPORATED, New York, New York　　　　　　1984 - 1990
Account Manager
Responsibilities:
- Sales of cosmetic line through three levels of distribution: manufacturer to distributor, retailer, and consumer.
- Traveled thirty-four states with average annual sales of $2.3 million.
- Conducted sales training meetings, seminars, and workshops for distributors and retailers.
- Created and designed displays, exhibits, and promotional materials for trade shows.

> **SPECIFIC FIGURES ENHANCE CREDIBILITY**

Achievements:
- Selected by Devon administrators to open select new markets with distributors and retailers in twenty-two states.
- Designed, complete with layout and copy, camera-ready Devon advertising.
- Implemented new product promotion, including product, display, and promotional material.

Awards:
- Devon Sales of the Month Award (nineteen times)　　**THE TYPE OF AWARD THAT**
- Best Sales Presentation Award (1984, 1986, 1989)　　**GETS ATTENTION**

CHRONOLOGICAL

MANNEQUIN MODEL AGENCY, St. Clair Shores, Michigan   1980 - 1984
Licensed fashion and modeling school and agency.
<u>Director of Education</u>
Responsibilities:

- Researched, designed, and authored three curriculum programs.
- Designed and authored training manual.
- Trained, managed, and supervised office and teaching staff.
- Coordinated and conducted nearly one hundred seminars and lectures to civic, education, and business groups.

> ACTION STATEMENTS REVEAL THE FULL RANGE OF ACCOMPLISHMENTS IN A MEANINGFUL CONTEXT

EDUCATION:

1980 OREGON COLLEGE, Medford, Oregon
B.S., Fashion Merchandising and Marketing

> SOLID ACADEMIC CREDENTIALS

FOREIGN LANGUAGES: French, Spanish

> NO PERSONAL DETAILS ABOUT MARITAL OR FAMILY STATUS

Resume Example #26: A retired executive seeking part-time consulting work.

ISAAC E. ELDER

25 Cedar Lane
Raleigh, North Carolina 27602

Home Telephone: (919) 555-0001

EMPLOYMENT OBJECTIVE:
To apply my extensive management, problem-solving, marketing, and interpersonal skills in the consulting capacity to selected sales and marketing organizations. [SPECIFIC]

SUMMARY OF ACCOMPLISHMENTS:

[ACCOMPLISHMENTS SUPPORT OBJECTIVE]

["PEOPLE SKILLS"]

- Doubled sales in capacity as marketing director over a three-year period despite a down economy (1989-1992).

- Redesigned and regrouped over one hundred sales/marketing brochures into twenty coordinated pamphlets that won *Marketing Age* magazine's "Award of Excellence." [VINTAGE QUALITY]

- Managed one of nine national sales regions which was consistently number one for twenty-one quarters (1974-1978). [CONSISTENCY]

- Active member of National Machine Tool Builders Association. Headed technical update sub-committee (1986-1992).

- Named St. Louis Business Alliance "Public Speaker of the Year" (1988 and 1990).

- Started St. Louis Business Alliance mentoring program linking over three hundred volunteer executives with high school and college students. [RESPONSIBILITY]

- Recognized as developer of effective sales representatives. "Salesman of the Year" came from my region three out of four years.

- Prepared, managed, and monitored corporate marketing budget exceeding $2 million.

- Developed and assisted in leading over two hundred sales representatives through a three-week "Sales Excellence" training program.

EMPLOYMENT HISTORY:
CROSBY MACHINE TOOL CORPORATION; Abilene, Texas
Marketing Vice President (1979-1992)

McDOUGLAS AND CARTY CORPORATION; St. Louis, Missouri
Sales Manager (1964-1979)

U.S. ARMY—Lieutenant (1960-1964)

EDUCATION:
B.S.—BUSINESS ADMINISTRATION, University of Kansas,
Topeka, Kansas (1959)

PERSONAL:
Married with two adult children [WORTH CONFIRMING AFTER HAVING REACHED RETIREMENT AGE]
Health excellent

[FITTING A LONG, SUCCESSFUL CAREER INTO A BRIEF BUT POWERFUL PAGE]

COMBINED

Resume Example #27: A high-tech entrepreneur employs a creative two-column technique to show individual but concurrent activities.

SIGMUND R. TIMEWINDER

9009 N St. N.W.   OFFICE (202) 555-7777
Washington, D.C. 20037   HOME (202) 555-1111

<u>SUMMARY:</u> Over twenty-five years of professional management and technical achievements.

| MANAGEMENT | TECHNICAL | BROAD-BASED TECHNICAL AND EDUCATIONAL SKILLS |

MANAGEMENT

1991 - Present
President, DATA SOFTWARE INNOVATIONS GROUP, LTD. Responsible for budgeting, planning, equipment acquisition, hiring outside services (legal, accounting, etc.), marketing and production. DATASIG has changed work patterns and demonstrably improved productivity of such major client software development organizations as Ball Labs, Ballcore, and other major corporations.

1988-1991
Systems Engineering Manager, BUSINESS MACHINES INTERNATIONAL (Banking Office). Managed two teams of Systems Engineers, including technical specialists (IMS, CICS, MVS, SNA, Project Management). Planned branch office technical staffing and training. Interviewed and hired for my own unit. Recognized each year as one of top 10% of Systems Engineering managers.

1985 - 1988
Project Manager, BUSINESS MACHINES INTERNATIONAL (Financial Office). Designed and managed implementation of major teleprocessing network, which included the first SNA-distributed processors shipped in company history. Planned project and quality control, and devised new techniques for programming, testing, user training, and physical planning. Established program of "walkthroughs" to assure quality of system. This 250 staff-month project was delivered on time.

> BOTTOM-LINE RESPONSIBILITIES

1980 - 1985
Marketing Representative, BUSINESS MACHINES INTERNATIONAL (Financial Office). Achieved over 100% of quota each year.

1976 - 1980
1st Lt., U.S. ARMY. In charge of Signal Corps communications repair facility in France. Managed thirty-five civilian and enlisted personnel. Instituted new operating procedures that reduced number of deadlined items by 80%.

TECHNICAL

1989 - Present
Consultant to PORT AUTHORITY and TRANSIT AUTHORITY OF NEW YORK. Designed, developed, and taught courses in personnel administration and inventory concepts.

1986 - 1991
Consultant to BALL COMMUNICATIONS RESEARCH. Designed and developed business model and architecture for large distributed database.

1985 - Present
Consultant to N&WG. Developed and taught courses in technical management, project planning, testing, and QA. Established QA organization. Defined development methodologies and tools for corporate standards.

1986 - 1988
Senior Instructor, BUSINESS MACHINES INTERNATIONAL SYSTEMS SCIENCE INSTITUTE. Designed and taught management and software engineering courses to senior data processing management and staff of major customers.

1986 - 1988
Adjunct Professor, GRADUATE SCHOOL OF BUSINESS, FAIRLEIGH DICKENSON UNIVERSITY. Taught MBA program courses: Managing Data Processing (for DP professionals) and Informations Systems (for non-DP executives).

1981-1983
Senior Systems Engineer, BUSINESS MACHINES INTERNATIONAL (Financial Branch Office). Provided technical support for all facets of data processing, including hardware configuration, software generation, DB/DC design, programming, and operations.

1980 - 1981
Staff Instructor, BUSINESS MACHINES INTERNATIONAL ADVANCED EDUCATION CENTER. Developed and taught OS internals courses.

CHRONOLOGICAL

Resume Example #27 continued.

SIGMUND R. TIMEWINDER
Page 2

EDUCATION and HONORS

Business Machines International Management School   M.A. degree in Mathematics, 1984
Business Machines International Systems Research Institute   B.S. degree (cum laude) in
Mathematics, 1976

University of Connecticut (Mathematics major)   Elected member of Sigma Xi,
National Science Honorary Society

Cornell University (Mathematics major)   Elected member of M.A.A.,
Mathematical Association of
America

> STRONG ACADEMIC
> CREDENTIALS

PROFESSIONAL AFFILIATIONS: AMA, DPMA, IEEE, ACM, ICCA, ASM
PUBLICATIONS: "Adding an End-of-File Marker,"
Exchange of IBM PC Information, July 1992

> APPROPRIATE TO THE
> PROFESSION

AVAILABLE HARDWARE: IBM PC/AT with capability to network with UNIX host.

> SHOWS ABILITY TO WORK
> OFF-SITE

Resume Example #28: *A recent graduate who is light on experience but shows an impressive list of achievements.*

HUGO LIGHTLY
22 Story Avenue
Lancaster, Pennsylvania 28717
(606) 555-1111

—— EDUCATION ——

B.A.; Penn State University, August 1995
Communications (emphasis on Management), with additional major in Psychology
Junior and Senior GPA: 3.7: Overall GPA: 3.3
Plan to obtain an MBA

—— SELECTED ACHIEVEMENTS ——

- Scored in the *top three percent* of all graduating college seniors in the United States on the GMAT (GRADUATE MANAGEMENT ADMISSIONS TEST) and in the *top five percent* on the analytical/problem solving abilities portion of the GRE (GRADUATE RECORDS EXAMINATION).
- Elected by 104 residents to position as Hall President, Hershey Residence Hall, Penn State University, 1992-1993.
- Excellent writing ability as demonstrated by a 3.5 GPA in writing classes, 95% average on senior year term papers, and an entry in school creative writing annual.
- Chosen to be Research Assistant within School of Communications, Spring 1992. Chosen as Teaching Assistant for Summer, 1993.
- Member of the Dean's List at PSU three times (3.5 GPA) while carrying an above-average course load.
- State Finalist in Radio Broadcasting for two consecutive years while member of Varsity Forensics team.
- Excellent knowledge of and working experience with WordPerfect and Microsoft Excel, Works, and Word.
- German speaking, reading, and writing ability after four years of high school and two years of college-level German courses.

—— EXPERIENCE ——

Penntec Research and Development, Inc.; Pittsburgh, Pennsylvania   **1994 - 1995**
Selected by Human Resources department manager to implement a Best Practices benchmarking survey and to assist in the writing and development of a corporate-wide employee training program in such areas as leadership, decision making, and communications. Solely responsible for the development of a ten-session leadership training program now in use throughout Penntec's North American operations. Position also involved compensation and benefits analyses, as well as considerable experience with WordPerfect, Excel, and Lotus 1-2-3.

The DH&S Group; Lancaster, Pennsylvania   **1994 - Present**
Currently acting as research associate doing marketing, product, and literature research for this organizational development and team-building consulting firm. Included in planning meetings with principals to help develop business and marketing strategies. Responsible for producing literature for the group and all word processing functions, requiring extensive use of Microsoft Office.

COMBINED

HUGO LIGHTLY
Page 2

Kelly Temporary Services; Harrisburg, Pennsylvania **Intermittent**
Offered permanent temporary position three weeks into temporary assignment at Kelly corporate headquarters. Assisted Accounts Receivables department manager in implementation of Total Quality Management program, and assisted Senior Account Specialist with Ford Motor, Philip Morris, and AT&T accounts. Other positions included responsibilities in team building, sales, accounting, purchasing, and customer service.

Straits Diving; St. Ignace, Michigan **Summers, 1991 & 1992**
Manager of a scuba diving operation with seasonal revenue of $250,000. Responsibilities included overall management of finances, retail sales, charter operation, purchasing, community relations, and dive instruction. Store revenue and customer base each grew by nearly 20% during this period despite a local and nation recession.

Resume Example #29: *A highly experienced senior executive sums up his experience concisely.*

E. X. PERIENCE
343 The High Road
New Route, Pennsylvania 19400
(610) 555-9673

Executive with twenty years of experience in service companies, including turnarounds, mergers and acquisitions, systems development, marketing, and sales, who took a company from a $1 million loss to a $1.3 million profit with sales increasing by $19 million.

CAREER SUMMARY

Proven leadership in sales, marketing, customer service, and public relations; public speaker/guest lecturer. Team motivator with ability to recruit, build, and retain staff. Managed staffs from forty-five to five hundred associates. Past and present member of Board of Directors of fourteen organizations of which six are system development/integration companies. **Bachelor of Science degree in Management from Michigan State University (1973).** Graduate study at University of Texas at Arlington.

PROFESSIONAL HIGHLIGHTS

- Directed private investment/corporate development group through three acquisitions and four refinancings; sales exceeded $300 million.
- Created alliance of four data communications corporations to form $90 million sales organization.
- Acquired two computer service companies.
- Secured major long-term facilities management contracts.
- Significant contributor in reduction of operating losses of $6.2 million to $1.5 million to break even in two years.

Hands-on operations, product management, and systems management experience resulting in increased profitability.

- Developed client/server and mainframe software products for national marketplace in credit card collections, loan origination, loan tracking, float management service, and national check processing company utilizing image capture technology.
- Directed successful portation of software package to new platform generating new sales. Sixty person-year effort.
- Re-engineered major West Coast bank's cash management services. Benefits exceeded $10 million annually.
- Organized functional departments into business units.
- Developed multiple strategic product plans including technology and new markets.
- Managed computer services company with five locations.
- Project management of multiple engagements that exceeded 100 person-years.
- Purchased and administered over $220 million in capital equipment and software contracts.
- Managed and controlled over 1,200 application conversions including four international installations.
- Planned, designed, and constructed a state-of-the-art computer center and headquarters facility.

COMBINED

E. X. PERIENCE

PROFESSIONAL EXPERIENCE

COOPER, HYATT, AND CO., Radnor, Pennsylvania (1993-Present)   Product Director
Consulting and systems development company. Subsidiary of Premier Financial Systems.

LIBERTY SOLUTIONS, Bryn Mawr, Pennsylvania (1991-1992)   Managing Director
Systems integration and software development company. Subsidiary of Quadrant Scientifics (NYSE).

HAMPTON ENTERPRISES, Ann Arbor, Michigan (1988-1991)
Hampton Information Systems (1989-1991)   **Chief Operating Officer**
Hampton Engineering , Inc. (1989-1991)   **President**
Hampton Enterprises (1988-1989)   **President and Chief Operating Officer**
Private investment/corporate development company owned by Charles A. Hampton, Founder of Hampton Publishing and Hampton Financial. Interests in network integration, distribution, technology park development.

GLOBAL DATA CORPORATION, Auburn Hills, Michigan (1978-1988)
(1979-1988)   **Vice President, General Manager and Director**
(1978)   **Director of Systems and Programming**
Financial services facilities management, automated services and software development firm. Subsidiary of Global Bancorp, Inc.

CINCOM SYSTEMS, Cincinnati, Ohio (1976-1978)
(1978)   **Sales Representative; Dallas, Texas**
(1976-1977)   **Systems Engineer; Dallas, Texas**
A worldwide supplier of database and data communications software.

NATIONAL SHAREDATA CORPORATION, Dallas, Texas (1975-1976)   Systems Engineer

UNIVERSITY COMPUTING COMPANY, Dallas, Texas (1973-1975)
(1974-1975)   **Project Leader**
(1973)   **Programmer Analyst**
Major software supplier to financial service industry.

The Professional Profile of

Hy Lee Creative

1900 Adelaide Road
Wellspring, New York 10516
Phone/Fax: 914-555-1111
eMail: HyVIAC@abc.com

A Personal Management Perspective

Businesses face far greater competitive challenges today than ever before, due in part to the expectations raised by advances in telecommunication and information management technologies. Customers demand faster response to their requirements, with no lessening of the quality of their products and services. A company's mission-critical objectives, are to provide better, faster service, with continuous product quality improvements, demand technologically capable management. As Drucker says, the right definition of today's manager is one who is responsible for the application and performance of knowledge. I strongly believe that companies can improve service and quality while reducing overall costs only if they are committed to continuously adopting and using advances in knowledge-based productivity tools. The manager who is adept at building successful teams that accept and employ these tools will be a significant contributor to a company's achievement of competitive advantage and profitability.

Significant Information Systems Experience

Experienced in work flow and process analysis and the development of systems specifications, leading to the evolution of international operations computer-based applications. Supervised Request for Proposal development, vendor selection process, and implementation of the new applications. Experienced in systems requirements and administration planning in both UNIX and MS-DOS environments. Knowledgeable of Electronic Data Interchange (EDI) standards. Experienced in desktop publishing and graphical presentations, as well as paperless (imaging-based) document storage and retrieval systems.

An Experienced Educator

Instructor, Export Transportation and Physical Distribution Management at the World Trade Association of the Port Authority of New York and New Jersey. Guest Lecturer, Globalization Course, at Hopkins School of Design, New York City. Guest Speaker, Export Seminars, at Virginia Port Administration and Port Authority of New York/New Jersey.

Areas of Expertise in International Operations

Purchasing and Global Materials Sourcing

♦ Demonstrated ability to source raw materials and capital equipment internationally, including aggressive sourcing of equivalent-quality products from alternative suppliers at significant annual savings.
♦ Experienced in managing environments requiring the purchasing of a significant number of SKUs, across a wide range of materials, involving annual spot and forward contracts.
♦ Capable of negotiating complex, multi-party, multinational contracts.

Transportation and Warehousing

♦ Managed the strategic transportation planning process covering the movement of materials sourced in North America, Asia, Europe, and South America.
♦ Experienced in the negotiation for shipment consolidation services, truck and rail contracts, export air and ocean (FCL, LCL, NVOCC) rate agreements, vessel charters, port selection, and small package services.
♦ Direct experience negotiating public warehouse contracts, both in union (ILA, Teamsters) and non-union environments.

Customer Service

♦ Capable of establishing service performance objectives and targets, and their measurement.
♦ Managed multilingual export documentation requirements, including third-party, country-mandated pre-shipment inspection programs (SGS).
♦ Established and managed high volume order entry, expediting and shipment scheduling activities, as well as credit and rebate programs.
♦ Experienced in product and distributor price planning.

Experienced in the Management of International Operations

CONSULTANT, November 1994 to Present
Specializing in work flow and process analysis, and global logistics, procurement, trading, and supply chain management information systems.

GLOBAL EXPORT MANAGER
Pacific Supply Division, February 1983 to November 1994
Orient Express Export Co., Inc. (New York, New York)
The international procurement arm of South American Ltd., a large multi-national manufacturing company based in Caracas, Venezuela. S.A. Ltd. is a leading producer of beer, wine, and soft drinks, snack foods, milled grain-based foods, aluminum cans, and biotechnology-based products. S.A. Ltd. manufactures its products in ten Central and South American countries.

MANAGER OF INTERNATIONAL CUSTOMER SERVICE
International Sales Division, September 1979 to February 1983
Runnels, Maybury, and Company (Elizabeth, New Jersey)
The centralized international distribution arm of a Fortune 500 manufacturer of institutional medical, laboratory, and consumer health care products, serving customers in Europe, Asia, and Latin America.

EXPORT MANAGER, May 1978 to September 1979
Lansdonne Incorporated (Princeton, New Jersey)
A manufacturing company specializing in precision valves and fittings for the process and instrumentation industries, including nuclear applications.

OVERSEAS SERVICES SUPPORT MANAGER, January 1976 to May 1978
Global Marine Contractors, Inc. (Baltimore, Maryland)
A large offshore oil field diving services and underwater construction company, contracting with major international oil exploration companies.

SUPPLY OFFICER, United States Marine Corps
May 1972 to December 1975. Honorably discharged.

B.A. (Psychology), New York University, New York, 1972 (Honors)

COMBINED

Resume Example #31: A consultant's resume—additional pages for publications are always acceptable.

ARTHUR D. ROSENBERG

---

250 Gorge Road
Cliffside Park, New Jersey 07010

phone: (201) 941-5904
FAX: (201) 941-4166

PROJECT LEADER / ANALYST / TRAINER / DOCUMENTATION SPECIALIST

| THIS LETS US KNOW WHAT IS TO FOLLOW |

Business Analysis
Training for End Users and Trainers
User/Technical/Instructional Manuals

SERVICE

| STRONG, CONFIDENT STATEMENT |

Analyzing and translating business requirements into software applications; producing accurate and readable documentation; designing and conducting training programs; RFP's and proposals.

SOFTWARE

MS Word & Word for Windows, Multimate, PageMaker, Word Perfect, WordStar, Flow Charting, Lotus 1-2-3, TSO/SPF/ICCF/IBM System 38 editors.

PROFESSIONAL ACCOMPLISHMENTS

- Hired and managed team of eight consultants in testing, documenting, and training customized JD Edwards A/R installation for major media corporation. Organized and conducted complex testing and training schedules throughout system implementation. Member of project management team.
- Analyzed and documented on-line systems for leading cable communications firm.
- Created training plan and manuals, and conducted training classes for clerical, managerial, and executive staff of New York City public sector organization.
- Documented timekeeping system and conducted training classes for police, tolls, airport, and professional staff of local interstate agency.
- Analyzed and rewrote large portion of customized methodology, based on Catalyst (CSC Partners) and Method/l (Arthur Anderson), for large international corporation.
- Documented inventory/order processing/distribution/billing system for a manufacturer of consumer goods and industrial chemical products.
- On-site project leader of group creating system and user documentation for IDMS order processing, accounts receivable, inventory control, and customer/product/ warehouse/database/security maintenance systems.
- Off-site project leader of two teams creating user documentation and training materials, and conducting user/instructor training classes, for the timekeeping and inventory control systems of two major public sector organizations.
- Analyzed and documented functional needs of major payroll and personnel departments; advised technical team on modifications to leading DB2 payroll/personnel package; designed user forms, documented system, provided on-line training.
- Wrote System Requirements Study/RFP for large contractor.
- Documented major transportation system, including user and training manuals; conducted classes for instructors.

| GOOD ACTION WORDS AND STATEMENTS |

FUNCTIONAL

CLIENTS

Analyzed and documented a wide variety of applications; conducted classes and training seminars in PC hardware and software, mainframe applications and methodology to clerical, managerial, and technical staff at:

The Port Authority of New York and New Jersey	Viacom/MTV
Cubic Automatic Revenue Collection Group	Rava Systems
Morgan Guaranty and Trust Company	Deutsche Bank
Teleport Communications Group	Purolator Courier
New York City Housing Authority	John Wiley & Sons
New York City Transit Authority	Delmar Publishers
American International Group	Marsh & McLennan
U.S. Department of Education	Paramount Pictures
Marine Computer Enterprises	Information Science
Univ. of Stockholm (Sweden)	Union College (N.J.)
Paladyne Software Systems	Berlitz School (Paris)
McGraw-Hill Book Company	United Parcel Service
Comerica - Detroit Bank	AT&T - Bell Labs

> SUGGESTS THAT THERE WERE EVEN MORE

RELATED ACHIEVEMENTS

- Editor, INTERFACE - monthly newsletter, Independent Computer Consultants Association (ICCA), NY/NJ Chapter.
- Directed marketing activities for two international publishers of technical and educational materials.
- Supervised multinational staff at United Nations agency in Geneva, Switzerland.
- Published college mathematics and business textbooks.
- Translated foreign language technical and promotional materials for the 1968 Grenoble Winter Olympic Games.

EDUCATION

M.A., English, French - University of Grenoble, France
B.A., Psychology - University of California at Los Angeles

PROFESSIONAL ASSOCIATIONS

ICCA - Independent Computer Consultants Association
APCA - Academy of Professional Consultants & Advisors
The Authors Guild
The Authors League

> RELEVANT AFFILIATIONS

FOREIGN LANGUAGES

French [bilingual], Spanish [fluent], German, Italian, and Swedish [conversational]

Resume Example #31 continued.

PUBLICATIONS

BOOKS

CAREER BUSTERS: 22 WAYS THAT PEOPLE MESS UP THEIR CAREER AND HOW TO AVOID THEM
Scheduled for publication September, 1996, McGraw-Hill Book Co., New York

MANIPULATIVE MEMOS: CONTROL YOUR CAREER THROUGH THE MEDIUM OF THE MEMO
November, 1994, Tenspeed Press, Berkeley, CA

PREPARING FOR A SUCCESSFUL INTERVIEW, the introductory chapter of **ACE THE TECHNICAL INTERVIEW**
1993, McGraw-Hill Book Co., New York

THE RESUME HANDBOOK
1987, Adams Media Corporation, Holbrook, MA
(2nd edition published in 1990, 3rd edition scheduled for 1996)

CHESS FOR CHILDREN AND THE YOUNG AT HEART
1977, Atheneum, New York

ARTICLES

KEEPING YOUR JOB IN A TECHNICAL ENVIRONMENT
National Business Employment Weekly (Published by the *Wall Street Journal*), February, 1987.

HOW TO BECOME A COMPUTER CONSULTANT
National Business Employment Weekly, September, 1986.

MAKING THE TRANSITION TO A TECHNICAL CAREER
National Business Employment Weekly, June, 1985.

RESUME STRATEGY
National Business Employment Weekly (3-article series), June, 1985.

HABIT UN-FORMING (INTERVIEWING TECHNIQUES)
National Business Employment Weekly, March, 1982.

We're confident these widely divergent resumes have provided you with a format and some fresh ideas that will enable you to display your skills effectively. They will encourage the interviewer to spend more time studying your resume, and less looking at the 244 others.

The successful resume can be thought of as an art form. We don't want you to think of your resume as a potential minefield, where the slightest mistake can eliminate you from the running. As these resumes demonstrate, there are countless ways to present your background in its most favorable light. There is of course, no single right way. Follow the format in any of these resumes, or borrow from several; the choice is yours.

Now that you've seen some of the recommended methods, a look at some of the wrong ways of writing resumes may prove instructive (and, perhaps, entertaining).

CHAPTER FIVE:
The Five Worst Resumes We've Ever Seen

If a good resume is a work of art, a bad resume is an envoy of self-destruction.

Included in this chapter are five of the worst resumes we've ever seen, selected from among thousands of misguided attempts at interesting potential employers. That they fail is obvious. We shall briefly point out some of their most poignant flaws, and we will show you how three of them could have been successfully rewritten.

PERSONAL: Birth Date: February 25, 1969. Single. Excellent health. Willing to
                     travel and/or relocate.

EDUCATION: B.S. in Business Administration, Central Michigan University, with
                     a major in finance, 24 credit hours; additional concentration in
                     marketing and economics. Overall GPA 3.1. Date of graduation,
                     May 7, 1985.

EXTRA-   Marketing Association, 1989, 1990, 1994.
CURRICULAR   Finance Club, 1990-91.
ACTIVITIES: Student Advisory Council, 1990-91.
                     Theta Chi Fraternity - Secretary, 1986-1990.
                         Rush Chairman, 1990-91.

INTERESTS,   Sports (golf, bowling, softball, basketball); leisure reading and
                     music.
HOBBIES:

WORK   1987 - Warehouseman for Leaseway of Westland, MI
EXPERIENCE: 1988 - Warehouseman for Leaseway of Westland, MI
                     1989 - Warehouseman for Leaseway of Westland, MI
                     1990 - Temporary Welding Inspector - Ford Motor Company
                     (after being laid off, painted exteriors of homes).

ADDRESS: Home: 66666 Fox Glen
                     Farmington Hills, MI 48018
                     Phone: 313-666-0606, 313-666-0607

COMMENTS: I feel that I am a dependable, personable, and hard working
                     individual who could be an asset to your business.

Name: Vincent Vaguely

Vincent Vaguely's vitae could (and maybe should) have been written on a 3" x 5" index card, the ideal size for recipes and other nonessentials. Although Vaguely seems to feel that he'd be an asset to our business, he has given us precious little data to support this optimistic view.

Now let's take a look at what Vincent Vaguely *did* include:

- *Resume*: We know what it was intended to be, so the label is superfluous.

- *Personal*: This information is unnecessary. If the writer insists on including it, he should have placed it at the very end.

- *Education*: Adequate, but poorly presented.

- *Extra-Curricular Activities*: Okay, but "Related Activities" might appear more grown-up.

- *Interests, Hobbies*: Who cares?

- *Work Experience*: Should list last job first. The same job need not be listed more than once. No mention is made of job responsibilities or accomplishments.

- *Address*: We finally discover where Vincent Vaguely lives. Of course, the address belongs up at the top.

- *Comments*: Unsubstantiated and unconvincing.

▩ ▩ ▩

CHARLES "CHUCK" CONFUSER   Telex: Smartashell
Easy Street
Big Town, NJ 07990

Statement of Position
As of July 20, 1995

"U" are current unit valuations of relative worth to investor.

ASSETS
CURRENT ASSETS
Abilities Derived Through Current Major Classes
    Technical Capabilities   U   55
    Spirit of competition
      (less allowance for cooperation)   90
    Communicative capacity   90
    Background in business courses   100
    Units from current major classes   335
    Leadership/Decision Making Ability   125
      TOTAL CURRENT ASSETS   460
Health and Physical Attributes   100
Former Education   75
Determination, Self-Confidence, and Self-Support
    (net of realization of dependence on others)   125
Goodwill and Intangibles   100
TOTAL ASSETS   U   860

LIABILITIES AND STOCKHOLDERS EQUITY
CURRENT LIABILITIES
    Amount Due Others for Maintenance of Interest and
      Self-Development   U   235
    Amount Due Work Experience   115
      TOTAL CURRENT LIABILITIES   350
    Long Term Debt to Supporters of Current Position   140
    Debt related to Mark 12:17   110
    TOTAL LIABILITIES   600
    STOCKHOLDERS EQUITY
    Common Stock   55
    Retained Earnings (to facilitate future development)   210
    TOTAL LIABILITIES AND STOCKHOLDERS EQUITY   U   860

Name: Charles "Chuck" Confuser

Believe it or not, such resumes as this actually *do* turn up from time to time. Chuck has obviously confused numerical facility with imagination and cleverness; a potential employer would not. This is not to say that innovation and creativity are negative ingredients in resume-writing perforce. But they must be applied judiciously and intelligently so as to complement, not dominate, important and clearly-organized information.

This document not only is *not* a resume, it doesn't come close to fulfilling the *purpose* of a resume. Even if someone took the trouble to try and figure out the "formula" (bear in mind the other 244 resumes waiting on the interviewer's desk), it provides no comprehensible basis on which to evaluate the aspirant's experience or abilities.

The lesson here is that a resume should provide its readers with relevant information; it shouldn't test their patience.

If all of this were not enough, the use of a nickname is another "no-no."

■ ■ ■

Eleanora Unsura
1404 Moore Ave.
Lincoln, MO 65438
(417) 555-1174
Social Sec. No. 390-92-6649

Level of Education:
High School Harper Woods High School 4 years
Business School Hallmark Business Machines Institute 9 months
Course of study Computer Programming
Specialization Cobol & RPGII Languages
Career Objective To Work Hard and become a good Programmer
Possible Salary $15,000 to $20,000 a year
Employment Experience:
Present Employer Whall Security Corp.
Job Title Security Officer.
Date of Employment 12/27/93. Current Salary of $4.25 an hour
Job Responsibility To Take care of clients property from Fire of Theft
Previous Employer Little Caecars Inc.
Job Title Store manager & pizza maker
Dates of Employment March, 1982 to November, 1983 Salary $180 a week.
Job Responsibility To make pizzas when busy and to do daily paper work.
Personal References: Billy and Jane Smith, 1403 Moore Ave. (across the street).

Truly Yours

Eleanora Unsura

Name: Eleanora Unsura

What's wrong with this little monstrosity? Almost everything! The major flaws are that it is grammatically abhorrent, poorly punctuated, full of misspellings, and unpleasing to the eye. It goes on to flout, destroy, or ignore virtually all of the fundamental rules of writing a successful resume.

To mention just a few specifics, salaries (past, present, and requested) should *never* appear upon a resume. If you insist on listing references, at least spell the name of your employer correctly. Finally, Eleanora's resume doesn't give the interviewer a chance to think about her background. There is no open space, relevancies and irrelevancies are intermingled, and it is completely lacking in structure.

Ms. Unsura gives us no idea of what she may have to offer a potential employer. She would be well-advised to solicit help in organizing and writing a resume with purpose and technique.

On the following page, we offer an alternative:

ELEANORA UNSURA

1404 Moore Avenue   (417) 555-1174
Lincoln, Missouri 65438

OBJECTIVE: A programming position allowing for professional skill development,
                    multiple applications, and potential for career growth.

EMPLOYMENT   Whall Security Corporation - Security Officer
HISTORY: Provide security service to a variety of business clients—hospitals to
1993 - Present   manufacturing concerns.

                    • Discovered electrical fire in early stages while on patrol at Parkcrest
                      Hospital, resulting in quick and easy smothering of fire and saving
                      potential loss of costly research equipment.
                    • Maintained perfect attendance record while employed at Whall,
                      despite working at least thirty hours/week and completing
                      coursework at Hallmark.
                    • "Employer of the Month"—Recipient seven times.

1982   Little Caesar's Incorporated—Store Manager
                    Managed $515,000 annual receipt, seven-employee carry-out restaurant.

                    • Reduced losses from incorrectly filled orders by redesigning order
                      form. This resulted in a 55% drop in losses.
                    • Appointed manager at age seventeen and while still a senior in high
                      school.

EDUCATION: Hallmark Business Machines Institute—1995.
                    Completed nine-month computer programming program with a
                    proficiency score on final testing of 92%.

                    Harper Woods H.S., 1992. Graduated within College Preparatory
                    Curriculum.

ACTIVE INTERESTS: Home computers, computer technical journals.

The Resume Handbook

Yes, this is the same Eleanora Unsura who authored the previous interviewer's nightmare. With some careful thought awarded her achievements, a new-found respect for the English language, some carefully chosen action verbs, and a logical format, Eleanora's resume has made a Pygmalion-like transition.

■ ■ ■

RESUME

I.M. Brusk
123 S. Adams
Correl, California 91106
(213) 000-0000

Department of Geography
California State University
80 State College Avenue
Fullerton, California 91106
(213) 000-0001

EDUCATION

1984	School of Business Administration & Economics California State University - Fullerton M.B.A.
1982 - 1986	Economic Geography Option U.C. Berkeley Ph.D.
1979 - 1982	Geography, Major - Economics, Minor B.A. University of Bristol (England) Special Honors

WORK EXPERIENCE

1990 - present	Associate Professor Department of Geography California State University - Fullerton
1986 - 1990	Assistant Professor Department of Geography California State University - Fullerton
1985 - 1986	Instructor Department of Economics University of San Francisco

CONSULTING

1992 - 1996	Urban Econometrics Co., Fullerton, Ca.
1992 - 1995	Market Profiles, Inc., Tustin, Ca.
1992	Orange County Forecast and Analysis Center

AWARDS, HONORS

1983 - 1984	James P. Sutton Fellowship, U.C. Berkeley
1982 - 1983	Thomas and Elizabeth Williams Scholarship, Glamorgan City Council
1979 - 1982	Special Honors, University of Bristol

Name: I.M. Brusk

What a pity to portray such an impressive record of academic excellence in such an unimpressive fashion.

This resume tells us that I.M. Brusk has earned an M.B.A., a Ph.D., and special honors. We can further deduce, with careful study, that the individual was promoted from Assistant to Associate Professor.

The rest is speculation. Has this seemingly intelligent person published? What courses and seminars has he taught? What are his academic and scientific specialties? What was the nature of his consulting? Has he any noteworthy research in progress? What, if any, are his goals? Why, we don't even know if he is, in fact, a *he* or a *she*.

Presumably, Professor Brusk is looking for a highly specialized position. However, there are other qualified people out there with Ph.D.s and honors of their own in competition. Given similar academic credentials, those whose resumes present them in a more interesting light are likelier to win the interview.

Our advice to I.M. Brusk is to rewrite this resume with the elements we've outlined in *The Resume Handbook*. It might look something like the one on the following page.

ISABELLA M. BRUSK

123 South Adams
Correl, California 91106

Residence: (213) 000-0000
Work: (213) 000-0000

EXPERIENCE
1986 - Current

California State University - Fullerton, Associate Professor, Department of Geography. Responsible for curriculum development for entire department covering 3,700 students annually. Personally direct ten department classes each year, including newly designed class entitled "Changing Weather Patterns - Dawn of a New Age."

- Co-authored "Economic Cycle Influences of Changing Political Boundaries," a highly acclaimed series of articles appearing in July-October 1993 issues of the *Research Economist*.

Selected as:

- Member of Governor's Council on Earthquake Readiness, a sixteen-member task force of business, academic, and government people assessing current state readiness regarding safety, economic disruption and proposed construction considerations. Youngest member of panel.

- Rated 96.4 out of 100 by nearly 750 students attending my classes during 1990-95. "90" is considered "outstanding."

- Developed and tested computer model identifying economic trends (i.e., unemployment rates, median incomes, others) caused by changing populations. This was accomplished during a consulting assignment with Urban Econometrics, Fullerton, CA.

- Conceived, designed and sold predictive voting model that pinpoints political voting trends utilizing demographics rather than polling. This predictive model has accurately predicted twenty-seven out of twenty-nine county races in 1973-96.

1985 - 1986

University of San Francisco, Instructor - Department of Economics. Responsible for leading one senior-level undergrad and two graduate-level Microeconomics classes involving 120+ students.

- Developed instructional curriculum for sixty-hour class entitled "Economic Patterns and Their Historical Perspectives."

page 2

PROFESSIONAL ASSOCIATION
American Association of Geographers

LANGUAGES
Welsh, French

PUBLICATIONS

1. *Hydrological Implications of Geothermal Developments in the Imperial Valley of Southern California*
   with G. George, R.H. Foster, and D.K. Todd
   Sea Water Conversion Laboratory, UCB, Richmond, November, 1985.

2. *1988 Population Estimate*
   with G. George and G. Britton
   Report on the Status of Orange County, 1988. Working Document No. 1, Forecast and Analysis Center, Orange County, CA.

3. *The Frequency of Social Contracts within a Time-Space Framework.*
   with G. George
   Submitted for publication.

PROFESSIONAL PAPERS

1. *Intra-Urban Interaction and Time-Space Budgets*
   with G. George, D. Shimarua, and P. Barry
   Association of American Geographers, New Orleans, 1992.

2. *The Soviet Concept of Optimal City Size*
   with G. George and C. Zumbrunnen
   Association of American Geographers, New Orleans, 1992.

EDUCATION

- Ph.D.-University of California at Berkeley, 1986.
  Economic Geography Option
- M.B.A.-California State University-Fullerton, 1984.
- B.A.-University of Bristol (England), 1982.
  Geography Major; Economics Minor. Graduated with honors.

We now know not only that Dr. Brusk is a she, but we've also gained a wealth of important information omitted from her initial resume. We've learned about her areas of expertise, that she has published extensively, and that she's popular with her students. Dr. Brusk, we find, has been appointed to a government panel; she is familiar with state-of-the-art techniques (computer modeling), and has had consulting positions with private firms (no "bookish academic," this Dr. Brusk). Without any exaggeration, she has turned a limp and lifeless resume into one that will demand its share of recognition in a fiercely competitive market.

RESUME
OF
BART BRAMBLEBUSH

RESIDENCE:

808 Hopkins Drive East
Administration
Windsor, Ontario

OFFICE:

Graduate School of Business

The University of Windsor
Windsor, Ontario

PROFESSIONAL EXPERIENCE:

1988 to Present	The University of Windsor Windsor, Ontario	
	1990 to Present	Director of Placement Graduate School of Business Administration
	1988 to 1990	Director, BBA Internship Program Dearborn, Michigan Campus
1984 to 1988	Substitute Teacher Windsor Public Schools Windsor, Ontario	
1980 to 1984	Training Manager Hespin & Marquette Windsor, Ontario	
1976 to 1980	Home Economics Teacher Weaton Public Schools Weaton, Ontario	

EDUCATION:

University of Windsor, Windsor, Ontario; Master of Business Administration, 1982. Major:
Industrial Relations

University of Buffalo, Buffalo, New York; Bachelor of Science, 1980. Major: Secondary Education

EXCELLENT REFERENCES AVAILABLE UPON REQUEST

Name: Bart Bramblebush

The preceding resume is probably the most frequent, and thus typical, form of resume failure we've encountered. At first glance, it may not seem so bad. In fact, you may be saying, "Gee, that looks like my resume!"

Indeed, Bramblebush's offering is not as obviously awful as some of the preceding examples of bad resumes. Its failure is more subtle and insidious, which is why we consider it more dangerous than the others. The problem isn't what you see, but rather what you don't.

At second glance, this sad excuse for a resume might be better suited to a footnote to Bart's career—it offers little more than the stuff of which memories are made. What, if anything, has he accomplished in his profession? Has he met with any noteworthy success? There must be *something* he has done over the years to interest a potential employer, but we can't find it here.

Other than where Bramblebush has been, and when, this document provides job titles, identifies itself at his resume, and promises good references to anyone who might be interested. Fortunately, we know Bart well enough to help him out of his predicament, and so we took the time to rewrite his notes into a solid resume. They hardly appear to describe the same person.

BARTHOLOMEW B. BRAMBLEBUSH

808 Hopkins Drive East   Residence (519) 101-0001
Windsor, Ontario 74R 01S   Business (519) 010-1000

PROFESSIONAL OBJECTIVE
> Attainment of a managerial level position as a Programs Director, Project Manager,
> or Section Head within a major university where my array of administrative,
> analytic, planning, and leadership skills can be fully utilized.

EDUCATION
> M.B.A., University of Windsor, Windsor, Ontario-1982.
> Concentration in Industrial Relations. B.A., University of Buffalo, Buffalo, New
> York-1980. Major in Secondary Education.

SIGNIFICANT EXPERIENCE
> MANAGERIAL - Successfully headed twelve-member, $540,000 annual budget
> placement function; increased enrollments 1147 over last four years at a 9000-
> student university.
>
> SYSTEMS DEVELOPMENT - Conceptualized and implemented computerized
> records system projected to save $175,000 in administrative expenses over next three
> years.
>
> FUNDS DEVELOPMENT - During two-year assignment as BBA Internship
> Program Director: established 359 successful corporate relationships totaling 577
> students, resulting in additional bottom-line impact to university of $205,000.
>
> PROGRAM DESIGN - Originated and initiated Student Enrollment Campaign
> involving promotional literature, student contacts at high schools and junior colleges,
> and direct mail: resulted in increase in enrollment during 1987 of 660 over 1986.
>
> TRAINING DESIGN - Designed Comprehensive Management Program affecting
> 275 individuals covering all phases of management from planning to controlling for
> major Canadian retailer.
>
> TEACHING EXCELLENCE - Runner-up two years in row (1972-73) as Teacher of
> the Year in a school district with 150 high school teachers.

POSITIONS

1988 - Present	Director of Placement, University of Windsor, Windsor, Ontario (1990 - Present).	
	Director of BBA Internship Programs, University of Windsor (1988 - 1990).	
1984 - 1988	Substitute Teacher, Windsor Public Schools.	
1980 - 1984	Training Manager, Hespin & Marquette Ltd., Windsor, Ontario.	
1976 - 1980	Home Economics Teacher, Weaton Public Schools, Weaton, Ontario	

Unlike Bart's first attempt, his rewritten resume shows that his flatly stated job titles were accompanied by significant managerial, fiscal, teaching, and operational responsibilities. In the first resume, his job progression seems sketchy and undefined. The improved version informs us of a logical progression toward the position he is seeking. Bart's new resume is an interview-getter.

■ ■ ■

We've done our best to convince you that even losing resumes can be transformed into winners. All you need are several hours of honest reflection (armed, of course, with your "resume tools"), an awareness of how your background can make you valuable to a potential employer, and a quick review of the basic resume guidelines outlined in chapter two. The rest is personal: choosing the format, typestyle, and layout that you feel best suits your background, and avoiding the pitfalls of poor resume writing.

Except for the brief final chapter on resume layout and design, this is our final word on successful resumes. The examples we have given you will, we hope, provide the tools you need for your own, unique profile.

However, this is not the end of *The Resume Handbook*. In the following chapters, we'll talk about design and layout, and then focus on the two essential resume companions: the cover letter, and the personal sales (or broadcast) letter After that, we introduce our brand-new chapters on networking and other job-getting and changing activities.

CHAPTER SIX:
Resume Design and Layout

It's no less important that your resume be pleasing to the eye than for it to clearly present the facts of your job history. This chapter will serve as a brief guide to structuring a resume that is graphically appealing and complementary to your background.

The first thing to consider is the paper on which your resume (and accompanying cover letter, or solo personal sales letter) is to be printed. An off-white paper stock may help your resume stand out in a pile, but beware of using pastels or darker colors, which look unprofessional. White standard business-sized stationery is always acceptable, although a quality paper stock may help with the overall effect.

As we cautioned earlier, try to limit your resume to a single page unless you have several years of experience and a variety of noteworthy achievements. The interviewer will appreciate it.

The next thing to consider is the method you use to put your resume on paper: typesetting or word processing.

Modern photocomposition typesetting offers you a clearer, sharper image, with a wide variety of type styles and effects, including italics, bold letters, and justified margins. Typesetting is attractive, but expensive.

We recommend word processing, which offer the most flexible approach. Resume files can be modified easily and quickly, stored, and targeted to specific employers or job openings. Word processing programs have come a long way since the first edition of *The Resume Handbook*, and the major packages offer a wide variety of typefaces and styles in standard and proportional spacing. In fact, the results are amazingly similar to typesetting.

The next thing to consider is the choice of typeface. You want your resume to stand out, not to compete with funeral or wedding announcements. Our advice is that you stick to a simple, clean typeface. There are, of course, many typefaces to choose from. However, we believe that ones like English, Times Roman, or Helvetica are best because of their simplicity of design and clarity to the eye.

Another trap to avoid is combining different typeface styles (i.e., Times Roman and Helvetica). On the other hand, those within the same typeface family may be combined to produce an attractive visual effect. For example, Times Roman typefaces can come in light, light italic, medium, medium italic, bold, bold italic, and several other nuances.

Having chosen your typeface, it's time to lay out your resume. During the design phase, bear in mind that open spaces make your resume easier to read. Avoid cramming your page(s) with heavy masses of print. For example, compare Eleanora Unsura's two resumes in Chapter Five.

Print as many originals of your resume as you need on attractive, letter-quality paper. Never send photocopies of your resume to a potential employer. They're okay for friends or employment agencies, but not the employer with whom you want to win an interview.

Another point is that the resume you mail may be photocopied by a personnel department, and subsequently passed along to other members of their firm. Copies made from copies can lose readability. In an emergency, some professionally maintained office photocopiers may do a good job, but we think it's better to avoid such emergencies by always having "perfect" copies of your resume on hand.

A final word: proofread your resume at every step in the process, whether it's typeset or computer-generated. Get a knowledgeable friend or colleague to help. Mistakes on resumes are embarrassing, unacceptable, and potentially they may prove disastrous. No matter how much you may have paid to have your resume created, you're the one who loses if it isn't right. So be meticulous—don't settle for less than the very best.

By way of example, look at the before and after versions of E. N. Trepreneurial's resume.

Before:

E. N. Trepreneurial

3000 High Expectations Way
Southfield, MI 48075
810-555-1122

CAREER SUMMARY

Twenty-three years of experience as an owner/executive of various types of companies including high technology, real estate services, and manufacturing.

EXPERIENCE

ENTREPRENEURIAL VENTURES, INC./COMMUNITY OF HOMES STUDIO, President and Founder
Entrepreneurial Ventures is a consulting company specializing in sales generation and growth (including turnarounds) locally, nationally, and internationally. Company manages all phases of marketing and management of approved plans. Client companies are start-ups through large international corporations that are in need of immediate attention and/or growth.

Company also arranges Venture Capital, equity financing, debt financing, mortgage, lease, etc. financing through Venture Strategies, Inc., an investment banking firm in Southfield, Michigan. Entrepreneurial Ventures assists automotive, manufacturing, real estate/building, computer/software, high tech, health care, robotics, electronics, publishing, consumer products, and service companies.

Community Of Homes Studio was a company financed and managed by Entrepreneurial Ventures. Community Of Homes Studio had the largest indoor showroom of modular homes in the U.S. (93,000 sq. ft.) , Featured ten homes that were landscaped and decorated in a village-like atmosphere with pond and waterfalls. Facility also had displays, mortgage companies, insurance companies, employment agencies, credit counselors, builders and developers, a restaurant, and day care. Activities involved housing financing as well as community affairs and parties. First six weeks generated 1,643 mortgage-approved buyers.

ENTREPRENEURIAL COMMUNITY HOMES, President and Founder

Manufactured housing company that erected homes in subdivisions
and scattered lots in eleven counties near metro Detroit.

ENVIRA CORPORATION, President and CEO

Research and Development Company specializing in aerospace remote sensing and image processing. Responsibilities included commercializing scientific developments with oil and gas companies, Department of Defense, medical institutions and other governmental agencies.

ZANADU INTERNATIONAL, Executive Vice-President and Co-Founder

Washington company that provided electrical and electronic components to the lighting industry. Responsibilities included strategic/business planning and day-to-day general management with over 500 people in twenty-four offices in the United States and London, England. Growth from start-up to $78 million in sales in three-year period.

COMMUNITY CONSTRUCTION COMPANY, President and Founder

Home building company that constructed over four hundred residential homes, numerous condominiums, and several light industrial buildings in Metropolitan Seattle. Responsibility was overall management.

VILLAGE MANAGEMENT CORPORATION, President and Co-Founder

First condominium property management company in Washington.
Customers included Hanson Homes, Hobbs & Cintas, Lewis & Lewis, and Allison Development. Managed maintenance, insurance, banking, repairs, construction, and developer relations. Company managed over 6,000 units and expanded operations to include condominium sales.

BENNINGTON INTERNATIONAL INC., Vice President

Marketing and Sales Manager, Ohio Division. Managed three used home sales offices consisting of over one hundred sales and administrative personnel. Also, was responsible for Bennington - New Town, a 61,000-acre development of residential and commercial property in Lester Township, Illinois. Responsibilities included planning, land development, municipal relations, serving on homeowners association, antique village (thirty-acre amusement and historical village), marketing, and supervising commercial and residential sales. Also managed two other land developments in the Bloomington area.

Sales/Marketing Manager, Bennington - New Town. Responsible for all new home building activities as well as commercial land sales. Duties included contracts, pricing, floor plans, home closings, builder relations, warranty, broker relations, advertising and promotion, and sales staff management.

After:

E. N. TREPRENEURIAL

3000 High Expectations Way
Southfield, Michigan 48075

810-555-1122

CAREER SUMMARY

Twenty-three years of experience as an owner/executive of various types of companies including high technology, real estate/building, services, and manufacturing.

EXPERIENCE

ENTREPRENEURIAL VENTURES, INC.   **President and Founder**
Entrepreneurial Ventures *is a consulting company specializing in marketing and sales generation/growth through local, national, and international sales organizations. Client companies are start-ups through large international corporations that are in need of immediate attention and/or growth (including turnarounds). Entrepreneurial Ventures manages all phases of marketing and management of approved action plans. Entrepreneurial Ventures assists automotive, manufacturing, real estate/building, computer/software, high tech, health care, robotics, electronics, publishing, consumer products, and service companies.*

Entrepreneurial Ventures arranges Venture Capital, equity, debt, or mortgage/lease financing through Venture Strategies, Inc., an investment banking firm in Southfield, Michigan.

- Company provides Staff, Board of Directors and/or Advisory Boards with national/international experience.

COMMUNITY OF HOMES STUDIO   **President and Founder**
Entrepreneurial Ventures financed and managed **Community of Homes Studio,** *which had the largest indoor showroom of modular homes in the U.S. (93,000 square feet), featuring ten homes, complete with landscaping and interior design, in a village-like atmosphere with pond and waterfalls. Facility also had displays, mortgage/insurance companies, employment agencies, credit counselors, builders and developers, a restaurant, and a day care center. Activities involved housing, financing, and community matters.*

- First six weeks generated 1,643 mortgage-approved buyers
- First in country to include layoff insurance for purchasers guaranteeing payment of the homeowners' day-to-day expenses; e.g., health insurance, mortgage, utilities, and day care providers
- Manufacturing capacity of sixty-two modular homes complete with site setups per week

ENVIRA CORPORATION   **President and CEO**
Research and Development Company specializing in aerospace, remote sensing, and image processing. Responsibilities included commercializing scientific projects with oil and gas companies, Department of Defense, medical institutions, and other governmental agencies. A subsidiary, a bio-tech company, was publicly traded.

- International leader in three-dimensional imaging of vision for the robotics and automotive industries.
- Leader in the monitoring of ice, icebergs, and their flows.

ZANADU INTERNATIONAL   Executive Vice-President and Co-Founder

*Washington company that provided electrical and electronic components to the lighting industry.
Developed strategic/business plans and managed over five hundred people in twenty-four offices
throughout the United States and London, England.*

- Start-up company that grew to sales of $78 million in three years.
- Sold products to over ninety foreign countries including England. 10 Downing Street
  was a customer.
- Rated as the fastest growing company in Washington.
- Research and development division develops products in conjunction with Motorola.

COMMUNITY CONSTRUCTION COMPANY   President and Founder

*Home building company that constructed over four hundred residential homes, numerous
condominiums, and several light industrial buildings in Metro Seattle. Company owned three
divisions, a real estate brokerage, a mortgage company, and an equity finance company.*

- Largest speculative builder in the state of Washington.
- Grew from a single real estate office to become the largest lister/seller of residential
  properties in the state of Washington in first three months of operation.

VILLAGE MANAGEMENT CORPORATION   President and Co-Founder

*First condominium property management company in Washington. Customers included Hanson
Homes, Hobbs & Cintas, Lewis & Lewis, and Allison Development. Managed maintenance,
insurance, banking, repairs, construction and developer relations. Company managed over 6,000
units and expanded operations to include condominium sales.*

- Expansion of the landscaping/maintenance division allowed service to thousands of
  apartments and commercial accounts.
- Janitorial subsidiary serviced in excess of 700,000 square feet of offices.

BENNINGTON INTERNATIONAL INC.   Vice President

*Consisted of a real estate sales office primarily for used homes in Bennington - New Town, a
61,000-acre development of residential and commercial property in Lester Township, Illinois,
that included an antique village (thirty-acre amusement and historical village), builders,
mortgage companies, marketing and commercial/residential sales, and a community
development company that developed properties in Puerto Rico and Florida.*

Marketing and Sales Manager, Ohio Division. Managed three sales offices consisting of over
one hundred sales and administrative personnel, New Town operations, and two other land
projects in the Bloomington area. Duties included planning, land development, and maintaining
municipal/ homeowners association relationships.

Sales/Marketing Manager, Bennington - New Town. Responsible for all new homebuilding
activities as well as commercial land sales.. Duties included contracts, pricing, floor plans, home
closings, builder relations, warranty, broker relations, advertising/promotion, and sales staff
management.

- Largest developer of year-round single family housing in Florida.
- Developer/builder of El Conqueror Resort in Puerto Rico.
- Owner of 40,000 acres in Michigan, Florida, South Carolina, North Carolina,
  Georgia, and Barbados.

CHAPTER SEVEN:
Cover Letters

Now that your resume is a polished gem, at least half the battle has been waged. It's time to hone the tool that lends your resume direction and appeal, the cover letter. After all, the potential employer, opening hundreds of resumes and letters daily, may not know what to do with just a lonely resume.

Writing effective cover letters is often underestimated in the overall scheme of seeking a new job. But cover letters can be an important key to the right doors. We'll begin with an example of how *not* to do it.

February 18, 1995

Arthur C. Reese
President
Southwest Tooling Research, Inc.
200 Mountain View Blvd.
Santa Fe, NM 80801

Dear Mr. Reese:

Enclosed please find my resume. After you review it, I am sure you will find that I'm a worthwhile and capable professional engineer who deserves further attention.

My current situation no longer offers me the challenge and responsibility level I demand. Because of this, I feel it is time to seek out another opportunity.

If there is any interest in my capabilities, you can reach me at (417) 555-4414. I'm positive you will find the time you spend analyzing my capabilities well worth your time.

Sincerely,

Ann Carmichael

Ann Carmichael

Would you go on to read the letter attached to the preceding resume if you received hundreds of similar documents each week? We doubt it. The letter leaves a lot to be desired: it fails to include vital information, lacks a definite purpose, and does little to entice the recipient to read more.

Effective cover letters convey a sense of purpose. They project an air of enthusiasm—regarding both the writer and the company for which the writer wants to work. And they demonstrate the writer's understanding of the company's goals, either by supporting or challenging them.

Objectives of the Cover Letter

A well-written cover letter meets the following objectives:

- It offers the job seeker an opportunity to personalize and target the resume to a particular reader;

- It allows the writer to direct attention to specific skills that may be important to the reader;

- It enables the applicant to clearly state why this organization is of interest to him or her;

- It opens the door for further communication and follow-through.

Let's examine each of these points in depth:

■ *Personalization*: The personalized aspect of a cover letter is one of its major strengths. A resume, by its very nature, is impersonal. When mailed without a personalized cover letter, a resume may create the impression that the addressee is one of several random stops along the campaign trail.

Address your cover letter to a specific individual within the target organization, preferably to someone who appears to have decision-making authority for the position sought. Most libraries will have a variety of research aids such as trade journals, Standard & Poor's *Register of Corporations, Directors, and Executives*, Dun & Bradstreet's *Million Dollar Directory*, and other sources. Make a list of specific individuals within target organizations. If you aren't sure who's who, call the company to verify your target's name and title.

■ *Directing Attention to a Skill*: The ultimate question that job seekers need to answer is, "What can you do for us?" Its importance during the prospecting phase should not be overlooked. The cover letter enables you to highlight or draw attention to a particular skill or accomplishment that has meaning to the organization in question. Its inclusion in the cover letter communicates some important information: That you've researched the company, identified their needs, and can fulfill them. In short, it says, "Here I am, the employee you've been waiting for!"

- *Clear Statement Indicating Reason for Interest*: This objective is the flip side of the above. Whereas before you highlighted a specific skill, here you indicate where in the target organization your skill can best be put to use. Once again, you reinforce the image of being knowledgeable and industry-wise.

- *Control and Follow-through*: This objective allows you to initiate the exchange of further communication. Much of the job search process lies outside the applicant's control. Some control, however, is gained when you mail (and follow up) a resume and cover letter.

Now that the objectives of the cover letter have brought into focus, let's return to the opening example and review its content.

The previous cover letter accomplishes very little. On the following page we show how the original letter might have been reworded.

February 18, 1995

Arthur C. Reese
President
Southwest Tooling Research, Inc.
200 Mountain View Blvd.
Santa Fe, New Mexico 80801

Dear Mr. Reese:

I read with great interest a recent article in *Engineering Today* entitled "Southwest Tooling's Push to Maintain Engineering Excellence." The article talked of your plans to increase your Engineering Research Lab Team. This emphasis on expansion appears to be a positive sign of Southwest's continuing dedication to quality service. I am extremely intrigued by the team research concept you have developed. The motivating force within a research team offers each member a sense of pride and accomplishment.

The enclosed resume demonstrates my extensive, long-range commitment to tooling research. You will also notice my own experience working with the team research concept. It goes without saying that you are looking for the best possible people to staff your growing organization. I feel I can offer you and Southwest Tooling substantial experience and the high degree of excellence that you need.

I look forward to meeting you to discuss your open position. I will call you during the early part of the week of March 22, to arrange an interview and to discuss my possible involvement with Southwest Tooling.

Sincerely,

Ann Carmichael

Ann Carmichael

This version puts all four major objectives to use, stressing the writer's strengths and value (tooling research and team experience). It answers the two important questions: "Why are you sending us your resume?" and, "What value can you offer us?" and closes with the promise to follow up with a phone call. The overall tone is enthusiastic and informative, without being wordy or overstated. Here's another good example.

October 28, 1995

Mr. Robert T. McPhail
Vice President of Marketing
Lencor Industries, Inc.
2002 Island Harbor
Fort Myers, Florida 20114

Dear Mr. McPhail:

I recently reviewed with interest an article you wrote in *Sales Management* magazine, entitled "Motivation Through Marketing Excellence." The marketing philosophy at Lencor corresponds to what I have accomplished on a small scale on my current assignment.

As you will note from my enclosed resume, my sales and marketing accomplishments, especially at Eastern General, favorably fit your "Marketplace Management" concept.

Because of my familiarity with your customer base and distribution network, I feel comfortable about my potential contribution to your growing organization. My experience over the last three years of increasing sales in my territory by 31% demonstrates my ability to succeed.

I will be in Fort Myers during the third and forth weeks of November. May we sit down and discuss "Marketplace Management" and my strong interest in your sales group? I will contact you the first week in November to finalize arrangements.

I look forward to meeting with you.

Sincerely,

William J. Adamson

William J. Adamson

Once again, each of the four objectives is met with a forceful and energetic style. The writer has zeroed in on his value and how it relates to the employer's needs. His approach is interesting and flattering without exaggeration. He highlights areas of his resume that are clearly oriented toward the job he's seeking, demonstrates a knowledge of the industry, and takes the initiative by stating when he intends to call.

A cover letter can be essential to the job search. It may not land the job, but it can influence how favorably your resume is viewed, or if it is viewed at all.

With this in mind, here are some examples of cover letters geared toward specific situations:

- Responding to an advertisement
- Writing to a search firm
- Networking with friends
- Covering your targeted market with a mass mailing
- Reaching consulting firms
- Targeting a specific company
- Contacting a referral

Cover Letter Example #1a: An ideal format to use when responding to an advertisement.

DATE

ADDRESSEE NAME
AND ADDRESS

Good Day:

The position of Chief Financial Officer, outlined in your advertisement of August 17, 1995, matches my career interests and is strongly compatible with my skills and experience.

The fact that your company is a manufacturer and distributor in both international and domestic locations is of particular interest, since these responsibilities coincide with my recent activities.

As a Financial Officer for an international corporation, I have considerable experience in directing the full spectrum of accounting and financial management activities. Specifically, I have:

* designed and directed the installation of an international data communication network for reporting sales and marketing office activity;

* initiated and designed data processing systems providing significant improvement in reporting accuracy, management control, and organizational productivity during a period of rapid expansion;

* directed the cash management and treasury function (including planning and investment of $47 million), as well as all the forecasting for four divisions and fifteen markets.

Additional accomplishments are listed in the enclosed resume

My academic qualifications include an M.B.A. and an undergraduate degree in finance. I have been a C.P.A. in the state of Ohio since 1978.

I believe that a personal meeting would be worthwhile. You can contact me during the day at (216) 123-0000 or by letter at my home address.

Sincerely,

Andrew Applicant

Andrew Applicant

Cover Letter Example #1b: *An innovative response to an advertisement.*

DATE

ADDRESSEE NAME
AND ADDRESS

Dear Ms. Employer:

This is in reply to your advertisement for an Accounting Representative in the *Sunday Star Ledger* on January 7, 1995. As the following comparison shows, my experience and background match this position's requirements closely.

YOUR REQUIREMENTS	MY QUALIFICATIONS
Three to five years accounting experience.	Five years in-depth accounting experience. Achieved impressive results by reducing costs and improving inventory control for three years. Administered five-member staff.
Strong communication skills.	Proven excellence in ongoing oral and written communications with clients and staff. Developed and presented workshops and classes. Prepared operational procedures and accounting manuals.
Knowledge of accounting systems.	Experienced in day-to-day processing of complex accounting systems. This includes generating input and analyzing output. Updated existing system to provide greater operational flexibility.

I would appreciate the opportunity to discuss the position with you personally. I will call you next week to see when we can arrange a meeting.

Sincerely,

Andrea Applicant

Andrea Applicant

Cover Letter Example #1c: Responding aggressively to an advertisement.

DATE

ADDRESSEE NAME
AND ADDRESS

Dear Sir/Madam,

I am responsible for $42 million worth of business in five top consumer and industrial marketing accounts.

Your company is represented as an organization that would appreciate the special and unusual talents I offer. Do my expertise in marketing and sales, entrepreneurial spirit, and professionally assertive nature appear to fit with your objectives?

The enclosed resume will itemize my credentials as noted in my most recent performance review. My manager described me as " . . . an outstanding member of the Marketing Team who is recognized by her peers as one of the best."

Salary is something I would prefer to discuss in confidence.

I am looking forward to hearing from you soon to explore any mutually beneficial opportunities.

Sincerely yours,

Marianne Hopeful

Marianne Hopeful

Cover Letter Example #2a: A letter to a search firm.

DATE

ADDRESSEE NAME
AND ADDRESS

Dear Mr. Looker,

No doubt some of your clients are facing a problem common in many sectors of American industry: how to stay competitive and profitable in a fluctuating market.

Perhaps one of them is looking for a well-seasoned and broadly based executive seeking to continue a successful management career in the automotive components and manufacturing business.

My years of hands-on experience embrace a verifiable history of cost reduction, quality improvement, and personnel management with small to medium-sized manufacturers.

Some of my successful solutions included putting in motion a quality program (Statistical Process Control) to increase productivity; establishing controls on raw and in-process inventories to increase cash flow, and reducing absenteeism by implementing a point system for feedback and control. I've also improved manufacturing methods to allow direct and indirect labor costs-to-sales ratios to remain constant even as labor costs increase.

Here are a few examples:

* Instituted a system for in-house brazing. This increased first-year profits by nearly $110,000 and in succeeding years by over $200,000.

* Recommended the formation of a company, making new facility profitable and increasing the parent company's profits by 11%.

* Formed a tooling machine company, making new facility profitable and increasing parent company profits by 7%.

Further details of my career are included in the accompanying resume. Should my background fit one of your current client assignments, I would be pleased to discuss the matter with you.

I will call next week to follow up and see if there is any additional information you would find helpful.

Sincerely,

Samuel Seeker

Cover Letter Example #2b: Another letter to a search firm.

DATE

ADDRESSEE NAME
AND ADDRESS

Dear Ms. Bigtime,

Your company is well-known throughout the employment industry. I've also seen your advertisements in various publications. As the enclosed resume indicates, my background includes management of several insurance divisions. Some of my more noteworthy contributions include:

* Reviewing entire division's operation and reducing annual expenses by $300,000.

* Improving processing time in three areas by 20-30% without increasing operating costs.

* Developing and presenting several different training courses, with $100,000 in related savings.

I am also thoroughly knowledgeable in cost control, accounting systems, and administration.

My company's recent reorganization and staff reduction have encouraged me to seek a new position. Rather than accept a transfer that would not take full advantage of my abilities, I've decided that this would be an excellent time to look for a more appropriate and challenging opportunity. The company has agreed to assist me in this process.

I would appreciate the chance to discuss personally any position that appears to be a good match with my qualifications. I'll call you next week to arrange a time for us to meet.

Sincerely,

Melvin Mover

Melvin Mover

Cover Letter Example #3: A good letter to use when networking with friends and business associates.

DATE

Dear Charlie,

It must be six months since we last spoke. We had discussed our mutual interest in classic cars and forensics. I hope you're finding 1996 to be an excellent year thus far.

My career status is currently in the process of change. I have decided to leave Flaps & Zippers, where I enjoyed over six years of challenge and increasing responsibility. During the past year, however, I've reached the conclusion that I'd be able to contribute at a higher level—and on a more significant scale—in an environment offering an opportunity to apply my strategic planning skills.

I want you to be clear that I am not asking you for a job, nor do I expect that you may know where I might find one. Rather, my objective now is to expand my contacts and open the door to more potential opportunities. I was hoping to obtain from you the names of some senior level executives, consultants, and business owners who might be willing to review my resume, offer their perspectives on the market, and point me in the right direction. I'm especially interested in contacting a Chief Financial Officer or Corporate Planning Officer.

The enclosed copies of my resume will update you with my more recent accomplishments. If you find it worthwhile, feel free to forward a copy with your recommendation to a close contact.

If there is anyone you'd like me to meet, please give me a call. I plan to contact you within the next three weeks to update you on my progress. I'm looking forward to speaking with you again.

Yours sincerely,

Clara Callme

Clara Callme

Cover Letter Example #4: Here's a letter to use in mass mailings—for the bottom tier of your direct employer contacts.

DATE

ADDRESSEE NAME
AND ADDRESS

Dear (   ),

The marketplace is becoming increasingly competitive. New companies with new products, old companies with better products, and still more companies with aggressive sales forces are contributing to the struggle.

Perhaps you have developed concern in recent months that your organization's sales force is not quite up to this level of competition. Or you may have wanted for some time to enhance the competitive abilities of a satisfactory sales group. Achieving either of these objectives requires strong sales management at the executive level. This is my reason for writing to you.

If you are concerned with sales performance, I invite you to take a close look at my resume. You may discover some qualities you like. Here is a brief overview of my accomplishments:

Directed my company to become the major supplier of polymer resins to nine of the top twelve users.

Supervised the development of amorphous liquids to allow for deeper industry penetration (tripled sales in three years).

Created a productive, harmonious sales force, decreasing sales costs while increasing sales results (nearly 45% over five years).

Please feel free to call me at (818) 123-4567 if you would like to know more about these potential contributions.

Sincerely,

Sally Selling

Sally Selling

Cover Letter Example #5: Targeting a consulting firm.

DATE

Dear Mr. Clientrich,

Your organization has ongoing relationships with a large number of businesses. Consequently, you are likely to be approached concerning needs that your clients may have identified within their own environments for senior managers and professionals. Perhaps one of these clients has a current need for a sales executive. If so, you may find it worthwhile to review the information I've enclosed.

As Vice President for sales at Aggresso-Tech, Inc., I built a sales force and a significant sales record. In 1987, when I was appointed Sales Vice President, sales levels were at $3.3 million. By 1995, sales had grown to $28 million, with a 58% return on investment.

Under my leadership, Aggresso-Tech developed ceramic gaskets, which allowed us to dominate the then-developing market. In fact, we have become the major supplier to the Big 3 of ceramic gaskets.

Should one of your clients or contacts be in need of a successful, proven sales executive, I would be pleased to get together with you prior to meeting them. Allow me to contact you within the next two weeks to determine if such a possibility exists.

Sincerely,

Melvin Marketable

Melvin Marketable

Cover Letter Example #6: *Targeting a specific company.*

DATE

ADDRESSEE NAME
AND ADDRESS

Dear Ms. Placewell,

I would like to address the topic of cost-effective conversion of parts to powder metallurgy.

You have seen this market increase appreciably over the past few years. To expand your market share, these products must be made and sold worldwide. Setting up optimum arrangements for international marketing and manufacturing is a critical managerial decision.

I have recently achieved a great deal of success in solving this problem through the use of overseas licensing. An integral aspect has been the sale of specialized manufacturing equipment. The substantial profits derived can be used to establish an equity position in the licensee.

In Korea, our licensee paid us a 7% royalty on sales, in addition to an engineering fee; they also purchased $27.4 million in specialized manufacturing equipment. I obtained an option to purchase 15% of the company for $950,000. In France, $17.1 million of equipment was sold to our licensee, generating a $5 million profit. I was able to initiate similar programs in Italy and West Germany,

As an added benefit, I negotiated with all of our licensees for the exclusive rights to purchase their products for sale in the U.S., thereby benefiting from both their lower labor costs and our advanced manufacturing technology.

As an experienced executive, I am accustomed to P & L responsibility for a company with $80 million in sales, and have managed Research and Development, Sales and Marketing, Manufacturing, and Internal Operations departments.

I believe that with my experience, I can help you achieve greater success and explore new opportunities in world markets. Permit me to call you during the week of September 7th to set up an appointment.

Sincerely,

Walter Wordly

Walter Wordly

Cover Letter Example #7: Used to contact a referral.

DATE

ADDRESSEE NAME
AND ADDRESS

Dear Mr. Hopewell,

Barbara Contact suggested that I contact you regarding our mutual interest in loss reduction.

I am interested in securing a position in the Quality Assurance department of a dynamic, high-growth corporation where I can expect to be challenged with responsibility. Your organization particularly interests me because of its outstanding performance over the past eight years.

As you will see from the enclosed resume, Mr. Hopewell, I have successfully carried out a wide range of difficult assignments. If you're potentially interested in having someone with my background join your firm, I would welcome the opportunity to meet with you and explore this possibility further.

I will call you within the next two weeks to discuss a mutually convenient meeting.

Yours sincerely,

Rita Reference

Rita Reference

CHAPTER EIGHT:
Personal Sales Letters

The personal sales letter concept is too important to leave out of a serious guide to writing resumes. Not to be confused with cover letters, which introduce and accompany resumes, the personal sales letter (or *broadcast letter*) is a *substitute* for a resume. It is primarily used when writing to selected cold prospects rather than employment agencies, classified ads, and the like.

Because the emphasis of *The Resume Handbook* is on resumes, this section is intended as no more than an introductory guide to writing successful personal sales letters. We've researched and summarized the topic with a great degree of care, and hope you find this brief synopsis helpful.

Philosophy of the Personal Sales Letter

The purpose of a personal sales letter is to offer an alternative to sending out yet another resume. In addition, it allows you to tailor your experience to the specifications of a position and a company. This approach can be effective when writing to a large number of corporations where you hope to attract the interest of a key decision-maker, and to explore the possibility of a current or future opening. It is less useful when answering advertisements or announced openings, especially where formal resumes have been requested.

Like resumes, personal sales letters are intended to obtain an interview. They are better suited to exploring corporate needs that may not yet have been defined, particularly executive-level positions.

General Guidelines

Always direct your personal sales letter to a specific individual, not to a Vice President or other nameless title. If possible, avoid personnel and employee relations departments, for they are generally oriented toward existing vacancies.

Use standard business-sized stationery, preferably personalized. Type "PRIVATE AND CONFIDENTIAL" on the front of the envelope, or a secretary may open the letter and automatically pass it along to the personnel department.

Do not refer to specific past or current employers, and leave out any mention of current, past, or desired salary. Keep careful notes on all correspondence; be sure you have a quick, efficient way to locate a specific file when someone to whom you've written calls unexpectedly.

Content of the Personal Sales Letter

■ *Opening Paragraph*

Your opening paragraph is the attention-grabber; it has to capture the reader's curiosity and entice him or her to continue reading. Unusual, intriguing information related to your objectives is a solid bet:

- ◆ I increased the output of my department 212% while reducing manpower hours.

- ◆ I made a successful living for seven years by selling African coffee in Brazil.

- ◆ A R&D Director of a major manufacturer of electronic testing instruments, I initiated the development of four highly regarded products.

- ◆ How often does one have the opportunity to engage the services of an account executive who recently captured a $1.5 million contract from a giant competitor?

- ◆ My professors referred to my final MBA project in financial modeling (just completed) as "brilliant" and "innovative." One of them suggested that an organization of your prominence in the industry could certainly make use of an honors graduate like myself, following my graduation this coming June.

■ *Second Paragraph*

The second paragraph tells the reader why you are writing to him or her. It identifies the specific job you're aiming for, concentrating on a single, carefully researched objective:

- ◆ This letter is intended to introduce me and to explore your potential need for a bilingual petroleum engineer who is quite willing to relocate. If you do happen to be looking for someone with my qualifications . . .

- ◆ I am writing because I anticipated that you might have need of someone with my unusual blend of qualifications in biomedical marketing research. Should this be the case . . .

- ◆ My purpose in contacting you directly is to inquire whether you anticipate a need for an executive recruiter with a good deal of experience in the academic publishing industry. If so . . .

- *Third Paragraph*

This paragraph is calculated to create a desire for what you have to offer. You may state what you've accomplished in the field in question, or list similar functions that support the kind of job you're seeking. Describe outstanding achievements (from your resume) which directly support the job objective. Use short, direct sentences. Avoid imprecise adjectives like "incredible" or "terrific." Cite specific figures. Don't hesitate to say:

- ◆ I accomplished/achieved/succeeded in
- ◆ I have received six patents, with eleven pending, on . . .
- ◆ I saved my company $3.2 million by reducing . . .
- ◆ As Director of Marketing of a small company, I increased sales by . . .
- ◆ My architectural design was selected and, under my direction, implemented . . .

- *Fourth Paragraph*

State specific, positive facts about your education and other qualifications that can be verified. Includes dates only if potentially useful to you:

- ◆ M.S. (with honors) in Management from the University of Michigan. I majored in Personnel Relations, and minored in Industrial Psychology.
- ◆ In 1994, I passed the 10th (final) actuarial exam for New York State.
- ◆ I authored the 120-page "Guide to XYZ Information Retrieval" (published by XYZ, Inc., 1993).

- *Fifth Paragraph*

The final paragraph tells the addressee what action you suggest on his or her part, or what may be expected from you. Let them know when and where you can be conveniently contacted:

- ◆ It would be my pleasure to offer you additional details regarding my qualifications during an interview. You can reach me most evenings and weekends at the above number. I am looking forward to hearing from you at your earliest convenience.
- ◆ I hope to hear from you prior to June 1, at which date I am expected to make a decision as to whether I will remain . . .
- ◆ I plan to be in Chicago the week of February 2-6. In the event that you would like to arrange an interview during this period, you can reach me at my home (212/123-4567) after 6:30 most evenings throughout the month of January.

Then sign the letter.

To further familiarize you with personal sales letters, two well-written examples follow. Note that they are both one-page documents, a length we regard as preferable, but not absolutely mandatory. We do, however, consider anything over a page and a half as wearing out the welcome mat.

■ ■ ■

CAROLE CORRAL
133 Charter Boulevard
Berkley, Michigan 48077

Mr. James Masterson   January 1, 1995
President
Romar Corporation
3303 Euclid
Cleveland, Ohio 44114

Dear Mr. Masterson:

Employed as a Personnel Representative for an international, medium-sized insurance company, I assisted in the development of the corporate personnel department. With the use of a centralized system of recruiting, interviewing, and selection procedures, I reduced turnover 30% over an eighteen-month period.

I am writing to you because your company may be in need of a personnel professional with my two-plus years of experience, education, and training. If so, you may be interested in some of my accomplishments:

* Researched and wrote a comprehensive, eighty-eight-page employee handbook, which included corporate policies and employee benefits.

* Wrote corporate salary and wage policy, conducted salary surveys, and prepared and updated job descriptions.

* Administered company benefits program including insurance and retirement programs for exempt and non-exempt personnel.

* Wrote a comprehensive employee training manual for a non-profit health care facility; this was distributed nationally to other health centers.

I received my B.S. in Management with a concentration in Human Resources Management from Oakland University. I seek a challenge and an opportunity where I can learn and advance within the personnel field.

It would be a pleasure to review my qualifications with you in a personal interview at your convenience. You can reach me after 5 p.m. at (414) 555-0280. I look forward to the opportunity to discuss career opportunities at Romar Corporation with you.

Sincerely,

Carole Corral

Carole Corral

MICHAEL MECHANNICO
921 Marshbank Road
Marshall, Idaho 09117

Mr. Ira Azimov   January 2, 1995
General Manager
MacIntosh Engineering
1400 Comstock
Mahwah, New Jersey

Dear Mr. Azimov:

In the last thirty-five months, I have successfully designed, installed, and made operational a computer-controlled, visually-activated robotics system. This system has already saved my firm $275,000, with additional second-year savings anticipated to be nearly $560,000.

I am writing to you at this time because of my strong interest in your robotics efforts, especially in visual scanning applications. Your pioneering research complements mine and has prompted me to contact your organization. Permit me to list some additional accomplishments.

* Received the John A. Cartwright Award as Research Engineer of the Year, Stamford, Connecticut Chapter.

* Published article: "Lights Shading Activators in Visual Sensing Devices," *Journal of Electrical Engineers*, December 1986.

* As Director of Research, 1984, improved on-time completion of scheduled projects 39% my first year, thereby saving $135,000 in early bid placements.

* Successfully turned around an historically mismanaged, unprofitable production facility within eighteen months; turned a net profit, reduced 50% plus turnover record by half, and cut absenteeism by 61%.

* Redesigned three major assembly lines, reducing downtime by 115%, reducing scrap by 55%, and improving product quality by 35%. An independent audit firm has conservatively estimated bottom line impact of these redesigns at $2.2 million.

I received my M.S.E.E. from Boston University, where I graduated with honors from their night program in 1979.

It would be a pleasure to offer you additional details on how I may contribute to your efforts in engineering and robotics research. You may contact me after 7 p.m. at home (208/123-4567). I look forward to your early call.

Sincerely;

Michael Mechannico

Michael Mechannico

The lessons from these two examples can be applied to personal sales letters in every profession. Personal sales letters allow you to highlight elements of your background in a more personalized format, and to rise above the more traditional approaches.

Used alone, or in conjunction with a resume and cover letter, this technique can prove surprisingly effective if you do it well.

CHAPTER NINE:
A Few Thoughts on Networking

Why add a chapter on networking to a book about resumes? Because a resume alone has minimal impact on the success of your job search, unless it finds its way into the right hands. Networking is one of the best ways to reach the people who can hire you, and the most successful of the many job search strategies available. The weight of evidence suggests that over 50 percent of people who switch jobs find their new employers through networking. All the other job search strategies (employment agencies, search firms, targeted mailings, mass mailings, electronic networking, and opportunity advertisements) combined account for less than half of positions gained. This is why networking is so important.

Networking is an art form rather than a science. There are no rigid formulas for success, only general truths and guidelines that can help you get started in the right direction. We define networking as:

A planned process of gathering and sharing information, ideas, and strategies through agenda-driven contacts with selected individuals in order to expand your universe of knowledge and create an awareness of your capabilities and availability.

Let's look at this definition more closely:

" ... A planned process ... "

Here are recognizable steps to the networking process to bring about the results you want. The process is "planned" in that you need to think through and design—in advance—the approaches and words you'll use, and identify the people you need to contact to maximize your success.

" ... *gathering and sharing information, ideas, and strategies through agenda-driven contacts ...* "

Mark Twain noted that, "Reading thirty books on any one subject would cause the reader to be an expert on that subject in the eyes of most people." Networking is based on a similar premise: talking to a number of people who have experience and perspective in a field can dramatically increase your own knowledge and perspective of that field. Planning up front the questions and issues you'll raise creates your agenda. The term "sharing" is also significant, because becoming a resource of information and contacts for others may encourage them to go out of their way to help you.

" . . . with selected individuals in order to expand your universe of knowledge . . . "

The people with whom you choose to network depend on which area of knowledge you want and need access to. Your approach may require developing strategies for gaining entry to a particular career field or occupational specialty. If so, you would need to conduct your agenda-driven discussions with people who have an overall perspective on that field.

Example 1:

A recent mechanical engineering graduate is looking for a position in computer-aided design (CAD). Her networking targets might be:

Recent graduates who have made a transition into CAD

Engineers who are using CAD

Software engineers who design CAD software

CAD instructors

Writers, editors, and journalists in the CAD field

Example 2:

An outplaced corporate manager who wants to purchase his own business feels that a franchise opportunity might be his best course of action. He should consider networking with:

Current franchise owners—not only to determine their satisfaction with this form of business ownership, but also their satisfaction with the product or service the franchise provides

Business brokers who buy and sell companies

Customers, suppliers, and competitors of the particular franchise he is interested in buying

Business and economic writers who have studied, researched, or written about franchise ownership

Asking the Right Questions

Here's a short list of generic questions you can use to develop your own set of questions:

What caused you to enter this field (or industry, or business)?

What were your major considerations before entering this business? (E.g., supply vs. demand, changing technologies, changing consumer dynamics, potential earning power, training, or upgrading of skills.)

Would you, knowing what you know now, enter this field today?

Based on what you know about me (this is where your resume comes into play), do you believe that I have the necessary ingredients to . . . ?

Does my resume indicate enough experience to allow me to be viewed seriously for this field, job, or business?

If so, what might I add to improve my chances for success?

If not, what should I add or change?

Is there anything you would recommend I do to prepare to move into this field?

Are there any strategies I might consider to learn more about this field?

Are there any other people you think I should contact for additional perspectives on what I'm trying to do—just as you have provided today?

May I follow up with you at some later date to inform you of my progress?

Is there any information about the field that I could be on the lookout for that would be helpful to you?

The final stage of our definition was to " . . . *create an awareness of your capabilities and availability* . . . ." The reward for behaving responsibly as a person who conducts a carefully planned and agenda-driven networking program is to earn the friendship and respect of potential peers. Who better to form alliances with than people in your field of interest? Even if you do no more than develop a friendly relationship with your first contacts, your time is not wasted. Often, some of the best results from networking meetings come later. The business owner you met with may pass your name on to a friend, supplier, or consultant. The more people you impress with your planned approach, the more opportunities you can expect. The universe does truly open up for those who ask—but be sure to ask nicely.

There are also pitfalls to be wary of which can destroy the most carefully laid networking plans. *Avoid at all costs:*

Talking unfavorably about a third party. Your networking partner will consider that you may do the same to him or her.

Overstaying your welcome. Stick to a time limit. "I promised to limit our meeting to thirty minutes, and I'd like you to know that I intend to keep my word." The only time it is okay to overstay your visit is when the other person suggests it.

Arriving too early or too late. Always plan to arrive for the meeting with four or five minutes to spare. Earlier than that is boorish and shows bad time management; and arriving late wastes the other person's time.

Taking notes without asking for permission. Always ask—most people don't mind when asked.

Failing to summarize the ideas, suggestions, and other names given to you. This is the sign of a bad listener and calls into question your respect for the value of ideas given to you.

Never, but *never* ask for a job in a networking meeting. This faux pas means instant loss of credibility and will be offensive to your partner. Even if you are offered a job (or an opportunity to interview), it might be best to politely defer it to another time, e.g., "I didn't come to this meeting today with the intention of asking for an interview, although I certainly appreciate your interest. I would very much like to follow up with this opportunity as soon as might be convenient for you. Thank you."

By Letter Or Phone?

Both methods can be useful in setting up networking meetings, depending on your personal comfort zone. Of course, letters have to be followed up by phone calls anyway, so calling may be the most convenient route. However, a letter gives your contact time to consider your request, and it is a polite way for a younger person to contact someone who is more senior (see the sample networking letters at the end of this chapter). Here are a few pointers on how to structure a phone call:

- *Build a bridge*: "You are important to me."

- *Disclaimer*: "I want to reassure you that I don't expect you to have or even know of a job for me. Rather, I need your perspectives and ideas."

- *Your situation*: "I have recently left _____ and as a result I'm exploring a number of options within _____."

or

"I just graduated from State U with a degree in Art History. I'm exploring careers in art. Your position as a curator provides you with a solid view of _____."

Keep your call brief. Be honest, positive, and to the point. Ask for help or for a meeting if appropriate. Remember to say "thank you."

Sample Letter Example #1 : Asking for networking meeting.

PETRA A. PLANNER
1234 Park Drive
Troy, Michigan 48084
(313) 689-5432

Date

Mr. Jack Montgomery
Divisional Vice President
Armature Industries, Inc.
2777 Lapeer Road
Rochester Falls, MI 48091

Dear Mr. Montgomery:

Loren McMasters encouraged me to contact you because of the significant involvement you have had in strategic planning. Your comprehensive ability in assembling corporate resources into a coherent plan is very important to me.

I very recently left a strategic planning position at Kalco, Inc. As you are aware, Kalco, Inc. has de-emphasized centralized strategic planning by pushing it into the line. As a result, I was given the opportunity to leave voluntarily. This led me to the conclusion that I would have more to contribute at a higher level with an organization that still values centralized planning.

May I reassure you that I am not asking you for an interview, nor do I expect that you even know of an appropriate opening. Rather, I am interested in gaining your perspectives and ideas on those issues that may make a difference to me. Your thoughts on companies I might target would be helpful. Additionally, any contact you may have who could also offer additional perspectives would be greatly appreciated.

Enclosed is my resume as a way of offering you a picture of my background. I look forward to meeting you. Loren mentioned that you "wrote the book" on strategic planning.

Allow me to contact you in the next few days to determine when it might be convenient for us to meet.

Sincerely,

Petra Planner

Petra Planner

Sample Letter Example #2: Requesting a networking meeting.

Cyrus T. Switcher
1000 Petershaw Road
Marietta, GA 30066
(404) 920-1000

June 14, 1996

Ms. Charlene Cerlot
1000 Clark Street
Montreal H2 x252

Dear Charlene,

Our mutual friend, Greg Caton, encouraged me to contact you. He felt that your thoughts on the career move you made from public accounting to general management might help me in the transition I am contemplating.

It would be helpful to me to hear what opportunities and obstacles you faced when making this transition. Finding out how you overcame the perception of "once an accountant, always an accountant" would particularly help me.

I have known for several years that I need a broader challenge of general management in heading up a small to mid-sized company or division. Did you move to general management for this same reason?

Charlene, I am contacting you not because I want you to hire me or in the expectation that you might know where a job for me currently exists. Frankly, it is your personal experience in finding a job by re-applying your skills that I am particularly interested in.

Allow me to call you in the next few days and see if there is a convenient time we might get together to discuss this further. I look forward to speaking with you.

Sincerely yours,

Cyrus Switcher

In Summary

Networking takes practice. Your best bet is to begin with existing contacts who know you and may be more forgiving. However, make sure that these meetings do not turn into "old times" conversations from which you derive little value.

When you initiate a new contact, communicate your purpose clearly. Whether you were referred by a friend or associate, or found their name in a journal article or directory of some kind, identify the source of the referral and then ask for an appointment of specified duration (no more than half an hour). Tell them enough about you to enable them to decide if they are willing to meet you. Be polite and brief.

One final suggestion that has worked wonders for a number of our clients is to do your homework. In advance of scheduling your meetings, spend a few hours at the library to research at least a dozen articles of general appeal dealing with upbeat topics, solutions, and ideas that your future networking partners may find useful. These resources, which might cover technology, economics, human behavior, costs savings, customer service, and similar issues, enable you to produce timely and interesting references during your networking meetings. Imagine being able to pull out a relevant article and say, "In preparation for this meeting, I was thinking about how I might repay you for your time and generosity. By chance, I ran across this article that might possibly offer you a useful thought or idea."

■ ■ ■

Good Luck, Networkers!

CHAPTER TEN:
The Other 50 Percent

Six other strategies account for the remaining 50 percent of job changes. These include:

Opportunity advertisements

Employment agencies

Search firms

Targeted mailings

Mass mailings

Electronic networking

A well-orchestrated search is likely to use most, if not all, of these strategies in conjunction with networking. In our experience, the vast majority of successful job changers we've observed, coached, or questioned used networking and the other strategies in tandem. Your discipline, available time, and skill in blending all of them together is likely to determine how long it takes you to find a new position, as well as the quality of opportunities you uncover.

For people who are employed while looking for a new opportunity, these other strategies may be easier to put into action during non-work hours. Their advantage is that they allow you to cover the market with relatively little time investment, as they require minimum interpersonal contact.

This impersonal aspect presents a potential danger, that of in relying solely on the other strategies and neglecting networking altogether. We strongly caution you to avoid this lapse.

Strategy #1: Opportunity Advertisements

Today's job changers read the want ads less seriously than in the past. The popular view is that it has become a numbers game, with choice opportunity ads pulling two hundred or more resume responses. So why bother?

Perhaps for the following reasons:

Responding to an ad requires little effort. Unless you possess obscure skills, you should reasonably be able to locate and respond to at least eight to twelve ads each week.

Attractive opportunity ads are more plentiful than you think. Most job changers look only to their local daily newspaper for opportunity ads. But trade publications, association newsletters, and national business publications (most notably The *Wall Street Journal* and *National Business Employment Weekly*) are equally good sources. Most of the top fifty metropolitan areas also have weekly newspapers or magazines that cover the local business community. A day at the local library can be an eye-opener for any job changer. When you open the job section, we urge you to read through the entire run of advertisements. Occasionally, excellent opportunities appear under unexpected headings. This will help you to become knowledgeable about little-known or newly relocated companies. Also, you may spot some potential business opportunities.

No experience or not enough experience? Respond anyway! We encourage you to give any ad that interests you a shot. What does it cost you? Just a little paper, time, postage, and energy. If you have at least some of the requested skills and experience, your mix of unspecified attributes might snare some interest.

Blind Ads and Open Ads

Blind ads are those in which the advertiser's name is missing. Open ads identify the name of the company and sometimes the name of their recruiter.

Blind ads. The most common concern in responding to a blind ad is that it may involve a company where you could be embarrassed or compromised by having your name surface as a job changer. One way to negate this potential inconvenience is to double-envelope your resume. Write the following note on the inside or second envelope containing your resume:

> *"Please Note—if Box 123 represents the ABC Company, please destroy this envelope and resume unopened."*

This idea assumes that blind ads draw mail first to a box at the newspaper. They, in turn, usually forward all resume responses to the unnamed company running the blind ad. It has been our experience that if you ask that your resume not be forwarded to a named company, newspapers will honor your wishes.

Open ads. We recommend that you not address yourself to the personnel or human resources department, even if this is asked for by the ad. Instead, call the company identified in the ad and determine the name and title of the individual who heads the division or department where the advertised position falls.

In both cases. When responding to any ad—open or blind—do not mail a response on the first day the ad appears. Wait at least four days before you mail your response. The idea is to have your resume reach them when there is much less competition for their attention. Send out a second response about two weeks after the initial one, adding the following sentence to your initial cover letter:

> *"This letter and resume are my second response to your ad of (date). Please allow my double response to be an indication of my strong interest in your opportunity."*

Note 1: In no case should you send out either an initial or second response to a blind ad any time after thirty days from the date of the original ad. Newspapers, typically, will only forward responses for thirty days.

Note 2: We do, however, suggest you to respond late to open ads—even five to six weeks after an ad first appeared. Many companies do not even begin interviewing and selecting candidates until several weeks after running an ad. The admonition "better late than never," applies here.

Strategies #2 and #3: Employment Agencies and Search Firms

Employment agencies and *search firms* work for their corporate clients, not for you. Don't contact them under the impression that they will find a job for you. Their mission is not to market you, but to locate competent individuals who match their client's requirements. In reality, the contact you make with them merely adds you to the pool of people from whom they draw potential matches for the positions they are seeking to fill.

Which of these may be best for you? The answer depends largely on where you fall in the organization chart.

Search firms deal almost exclusively with mid-management through senior executive positions, commanding minimum salaries of $60,000. If you fall into this range, consider sending your resume to several search firms (at least ten to fifteen) that specialize in your field.

Search firms either specialize in your industry or field, or generalize and cover all fields and industries. They typically work on a retainer basis, with a portion of their fee paid up front. Typically, they are the exclusive source of candidates for their corporate client. These firms often act as consultants to the senior management of an organization. Their reputation is built on consistently providing their clients with quality candidates.

Employment agencies, like search firms, either specialize or generalize. The difference is that employment agencies typically handle a majority of positions paying under $60,000, covering entry-level clerical and administrative jobs up through senior technical and mid-management openings. Like search firms, they serve their corporate clients by finding suitable candidates, and they are not in business to find you a job. Employment agencies are paid contingent on finding a suitable candidate who eventually gets hired. Unlike search firms, they are not usually paid a retainer.

Ideas for Utilizing Search Firms and/or Employment Agencies

Timing is everything. Because most active agencies and firms only work on a few openings at a time, you need to match your skills with their current openings. Your best bet is to get your resume out to a number of agencies or firms. Start by sending your resume first to specialists in your field, and then to generalists.

Do your homework. Identify all the agencies or search firms that cover your skills or specialty. An excellent source is:

> *The Directory of Executive Recruiters*
> Published by Kennedy & Kennedy, Inc.
> Templeton Road
> Fitzwilliam, New Hampshire 03447
> (603) 585-2200

This directory offers a comprehensive compilation of close to 2,000 search firms and employment agencies. The extensive information provided on each entry should help identify appropriate targets for your resume.

Include salary information. Playing coy with firms and agencies isn't smart. It's best to be open, honest, and thorough about yourself. Your targeted list of firms or agencies can either help you or they can't. By communicating clearly your skills, experiences, and salary expectations, you are making their jobs easier. Here are a few ways to deal with salary expectations in your cover letter (pick the one that matches your situation):

> *"I'm very open on salary requirements at this time, as I am much more interested in challenge, opportunity, and a chance to work within the industry (or field)."*

or

> *"I'm interested in a position with a compensation opportunity, including salary, benefits, and incentives, in the range of $65,000 to $80,000."*

or

> *"Currently, my salary is $45,000. I am most interested in opportunities in the $50s."*

or

> *"Although challenge, opportunity, and the reputation of the company I join is most important, you should be aware that my total compensation over the last five years has placed me in the $76,000 to $94,000 range."*

Identify seemingly obscure skills. Both employment agencies and search firms make their reputations by finding needles in haystacks. They're in business to find people with unusual sets of skills. So include any attributes, skills, or experiences that demonstrate your unique combination of capabilities in your cover letter. Language proficiency, technical training, interpersonal skills, or specific project or client-related skills and experiences frequently make a difference in getting you noticed.

Communicating with recruiters. Don't call agencies or firms after a mailing. Again, they can only help you if you match a job they are currently working on. Your unsolicited calls may be seen as an unnecessary irritation. A better bet is to send out a second mailing three to five months later if you haven't heard anything from your initial mailing.

Bear in mind that communicating with search firms and employment agencies is only one part of a balanced approach. Relying on these as your sole source of opportunities is naïve, limiting, and often futile.

Strategies #4 and #5: Targeting and Mass Mailings

Targeted mailings are as different from *mass mailings* as a laser beam is from sunlight. Targeted mailings depend on concentrated, discriminating preparation for results. They emphasize quality over quantity. On the other hand, mass mailings operate on the principle that more is better. Like direct mail advertising, they depend on getting some response out of a large-scale, relatively undiscriminating approach. Only by understanding the differences between these two approaches can you learn to maximize their potentials. Let's start with targeted mailings.

Targeted mailings. This approach requires you to conduct careful, thoughtful research to identify who might be interested in your unique combination of capabilities. The more thorough your research, the more likely you are to make the right choices. You can also use networking to pinpoint good target companies.

Introduce yourself to your local librarian. Be explicit about what you're trying to do. Most well-stocked libraries include an impressive list of directories which you can use to source and pinpoint detailed information. Some of the better known directories include:

> *Dun's Million Dollar Directory* (Dun & Bradstreet). This directory lists close to 200,000 businesses in a wide range of industries such as manufacturing, communications, banking, transportation, chemicals, utilities, and retail. Each entry will include financial data, corporate addresses, and phone numbers, along with a listing of the names and titles of senior executives.

Moody's Industrial Manual (Moody's Investor Services, Inc.). Moody's contains entries on 3,500 companies listed either on the New York or American Stock Exchange.

Thomas Register (Thomas Publishing Company). A twelve-volume set of directories structured alphabetically around products, services, and brand names offered by U.S. manufacturers.

The Encyclopedia of Associations (Gale Research Company). This publication lists about 20,000 professional and trade associations. It is a frequently overlooked source of appropriate contacts, especially for organizations that match your skills and interests.

This list is by no means comprehensive; it's intended as an introduction to the excellent research sources available at many local, college, and university libraries. Again, the better your research is, the better your targeted mailings will be. You need all the help you can get, and doing your marketing homework is a great start.

Two additional research sources to consult are:

The Encyclopedia of Business Information (Gale Research Company). This compendium of business information documents the publications—magazines, newsletters, books, and handbooks—available on over 1,200 business-related issues and topics.

Directories in Print (Gale Research Company). This is the directory of directories. Want to find the right directory for your specific needs? This is the source. It lists about 8,000 directories.

Finally, let's not forget the computer on-line directories that are available. The big advantage here is speed. The information is available immediately in most cases. Some of the major database vendors are:

The Source
1616 Anderson Road
McLean, Virginia 22102
(703) 821-6666
(800) 336-3366

Dialog
3460 Hillview Avenue
Palo Alto, California 94304
(800) 528-6060

Orbit
2500 Colorado Avenue
Santa Monica, California 90406
(213) 453-6194
(800) 421-7229

BRS
1200 Route 7
Latham, New York 12110
(518) 783-1161
(800) 345-4277

In summary, quality research can lead you to companies, people, and associations that are closely aligned with your skills and career goals. To the extent that you are able to pinpoint quality targets for your mailings, your likelihood of receiving quality responses rises dramatically. We've included a couple of cover letters (#5 and #6, pages 114 and 115) within Chapter Seven to use in targeted mailings. When you review these, you'll note how the research information in the letter can demonstrate to the reader how closely you match up with their objectives.

Mass mailings. As mentioned earlier, targeted mailings demand precise research and thoughtful execution. A well-thought-out job search might result in fifty to seventy five targeted mailings, while that same search could also result in hundreds of mass mailings. Mass mailings require less work; however, due to the large number of targets involved, they often produce positive results. Based on volume and requiring considerably less thought than targeted mailings, mass mailings are best used by job seekers with broad skills who work in less specialized occupations. Middle-level managers might consider doing a mass mailing, for example, to all manufacturing companies within their region or a certain distance of their home. Controllers or accounting managers could conceivably work anywhere that requires their types of skills. College seniors starting out on the job trail with an interest in sales and marketing could mass-mail their resumes to the *Fortune* 1000. The objective here is to cover the market like a blanket.

Ideas for designing a mass mailing of your resume:

Start by obtaining a mailing list. You can develop your own list, which can be time-consuming (but less costly), or you can obtain one from a mailing-list company. It pays to shop when obtaining a mailing list. Two sources to start with are:

Polk Mailing List Catalog	*Direct Mail List*
R. L. Polk & Company	Standard Rate & Data Service
201 Elm Hill Pike	3004 Glenview Road
Box 1340	Wilmette, Illinois 60091
Nashville, Tennessee 37202	(312) 256-6067
(616) 889-3350	

When buying or using any existing mailing list, make sure it's current (less than one year old), and that it contains the names and titles of the individuals who head up the company function appropriate to your skills and job search goal.

Address your mailings to a specific individual whose title and responsibility match your search objective. Sales and marketing candidates should direct their mailings to the chief sales and marketing executive. Engineers should direct theirs to the head of engineering or manufacturing. Focus upon finding the best targets for your mailing. Never mass-mail to the human resource or personnel area—unless you want to work in personnel or human resources.

Maintain your mailing list as a record. Nothing is more embarrassing than to get a call from someone responding to your mailing and not remembering who they are, or that you mailed a resume to them!

Write your cover letter in such a way that it appeals to the largest number of employers possible. Take a look at sample letter on the following page and cover letter example #4 on page 113 of Chapter Seven.

Sample Letter Example #1: Mass Mailing Letter.

Your Name
Your Address
Your City, Your State #####
Your Phone Number

Date

Addressee Name
Addressee Title
Addressee Company
Addressee Address
Addressee City, State #####

Dear _____:

American companies need strong manufacturing leadership that inspires their employees to deliver high quality, low-cost products on time.

I have worked hard to be that kind of leader, and my customers, suppliers, colleagues, and employees would support my claim. My record over the last twelve years shows that I've built teams, raised performance, lowered costs, and delivered quality on-time! More specifically:

* As Plant Manager of a $60 million, four hundred employee high-tech stamping operation, my group was named "Plant of the Year" by *Stamping Technology Review*.

* While Manufacturing Director for solenoids and switches, I landed two of the largest customer orders in our history. Both customers placed their orders on the strength of our quality and on-time delivery record.

My Bachelor's Degree in Mechanical Engineering was earned at Ohio State University; I am currently finishing course work for the Executive Management Program at Michigan State University.

I'd like an opportunity to apply my skills in a larger organization like yours. I look forward to the possibility of discussing how I might contribute to your success.

Sincerely,

[signature]

Your Name

Enclosure

Strategy #6: Electronic Networking

A special note about the fastest growing communications format is certainly appropriate for those of you who have—or are about to—enter this brave new world. There are a number of commercial on-line networking services, such as America Online, CompuServe, Delphi, GEnie, and Prodigy, that carry career-related SIGs (special interest groups—also known as boards, clubs, forums, or discussion groups). Electronic networkers are able to read, respond to notices, or leave notices of their own. It is also possible to participate in "real time" conferences which allow you to interact with people from just about anywhere.

Some electronic networkers enjoy sharing information and opinions. Your questions about the pros and cons of working in certain industries or locations are almost sure to elicit some useful responses. We've seen requests for advice on getting jobs, technical information, opportunities in other locations, and part-time work, among others.

Countless local groups operate freestanding BBSs (bulletin board systems). Many of these are listed in the magazine *Boardwatch* (800-933-6038), by local computer dealers, and in libraries. *Online Access* is a journal that lists BBSs and more general information on the world of cyberspace.

Afterword

The infuriating truism that "everything is relative" can be—and often is—employed to defend the most eccentric, idiosyncratic, and at times, ill-conceived of practices and notions. In writing resumes, of course, what is good and what is bad depends upon what *works*, and what does not. Results are, in the final analysis, what count.

Certainly the element of chance may enter into landing a desirable position, as is true of every aspect of our lives. But a well-organized approach can minimize the random factors and reduce the arbitrary flow of circumstances of which we may be unaware.

Our guidelines and suggestions are thus intended as a modest contribution toward helping you increase your control over the factors governing a single aspect of your career: getting the interviews you want!

With this in mind, we've shown you the ingredients of successful resumes, with plenty of practical examples. Now you recognize the differences between:

- Relevant vs. useless or potentially damaging information
- Active vs. static
- Attractive vs. unattractive
- Attention-getting vs. dull and unappealing
- Cover letters vs. personal sales letters

You now know how to:

- Emphasize strengths and de-emphasize weaknesses
- Focus on career objectives
- Write an interview-winning resume

Some things, perhaps, are relative, but effective resumes are based on the purpose and technique of a carefully conceived strategy. We hope that *The Resume Handbook* has helped you to develop your own strategy to get your foot in the door.

Good luck!

The Adams Jobs Almanac, 8th Edition

Updated annually, *The Adams Jobs Almanac* includes names and addresses of over 7,000 U.S. employers; information on which positions each company commonly fills; and advice on preparing resumes and cover letters and standing out at interviews. $5^{1}/_{2}$" x $8^{1}/_{2}$", 952 pages, paperback, $16.95. ISBN: 1-58062-443-X, ISSN: 1072-592X

The JobBank Series

There are 30 *JobBank* books, each providing extensive, up-to-date employment information on hundreds of the largest employers in each job market. The #1 best-selling series of employment directories, the *JobBank* series has been recommended as an excellent place to begin your job search by the *New York Times*, the *Los Angeles Times*, the *Boston Globe*, and the *Chicago Tribune*. *JobBank* books have been used by millions of people to find jobs. Titles available:

The Atlanta JobBank • *The Austin/San Antonio JobBank* • *The Boston JobBank* • *The Carolina JobBank* • *The Chicago JobBank* • *The Connecticut JobBank* • *The Dallas-Fort Worth JobBank* • *The Denver JobBank* • *The Detroit JobBank* • *The Florida JobBank* • *The Houston JobBank* • *The Indiana JobBank* • *The Las Vegas JobBank* • *The Los Angeles JobBank* • *The Minneapolis-St. Paul JobBank* • *The Missouri JobBank* • *The New Jersey JobBank* • *The Metropolitan New York JobBank* • *The Ohio JobBank* • *The Greater Philadelphia JobBank* • *The Phoenix JobBank* • *The Pittsburgh JobBank* • *The Portland JobBank* • *The San Francisco Bay Area JobBank* • *The Seattle JobBank* • *The Tennessee JobBank* • *The Virginia JobBank* • *The Metropolitan Washington DC JobBank* • *The JobBank Guide to Computer & High-Tech Companies* • *The JobBank Guide to Health Care Companies*

The Adams Cover Letter Almanac

The Adams Cover Letter Almanac is the most detailed cover letter resource in print, containing 600 cover letters used by real people to win real jobs. It features complete information on all types of letters, including networking, "cold," broadcast, and follow-up. In addition to advice on how to avoid fatal cover letter mistakes, the book includes strategies for people changing careers, relocating, recovering from layoff, and more. $5\frac{1}{2}$" x $8\frac{1}{2}$", 736 pages, paperback, $12.95. ISBN: 1-55850-497-4

The Adams Resume Almanac

This almanac features detailed information on resume development and layout, a review of the pros and cons of various formats, an exhaustive look at the strategies that will definitely get a resume noticed, and 600 sample resumes in dozens of career categories. *The Adams Resume Almanac* is the most comprehensive, thoroughly researched resume guide ever published. $5\frac{1}{2}$" x $8\frac{1}{2}$", 768 pages, paperback, $12.95. ISBN: 1-55850-358-7

The Adams Job Interview Almanac

The Adams Job Interview Almanac includes answers and discussions for over 1,800 interview questions. There are 100 complete job interviews for all fields, industries, and career levels. Also included is valuable information on handling stress interviews, strategies for second and third interviews, and negotiating job offers to get what you want. $5\frac{1}{2}$" x $8\frac{1}{2}$", 840 pages, paperback, $12.95. ISBN: 1-55850-612-8

Available wherever books are sold.

**For more information, or to order, call 800-872-5627
or visit www.adamsmedia.com**

Adams Media Corporation, 260 Center Street, Holbrook, MA 02343

FIND MORE ON THIS TOPIC BY VISITING

BusinessTown.com
The Web's big site for growing businesses!

- ☑ **Separate channels on all aspects of starting and running a business**
- ☑ **Lots of info on how to do business online**
- ☑ **1,000+ pages of savvy business advice**
- ☑ **Complete web guide to thousands of useful business sites**
- ☑ **Free e-mail newsletter**
- ☑ **Question and answer forums, and more!**

businesstown.com